A primer of SOCIAL CASEWORK

A primer of
SOCIAL CASEWORK

by ELIZABETH NICHOLDS

COLUMBIA UNIVERSITY PRESS New York and London

COPYRIGHT © 1960 BY COLUMBIA UNIVERSITY PRESS

First printing 1960
Sixth printing 1970

ISBN 0-231-02406-1
LIBRARY OF CONGRESS CATALOG CARD NUMBER: 60-12810
PRINTED IN THE UNITED STATES OF AMERICA

Contents

Introduction

THIS BOOK is written for those who want to help people. Kindly individuals are again and again faced with requests for help in areas with which their particular professional education has not equipped them to deal—doctors, to whom patients turn with troubles other than medical; pastors, before whom are poured out secular as well as spiritual problems; teachers, to whom students talk about their difficulties at home; employees of social agencies, who have come to their positions with no special training for dealing with the varied human problems they face every day. An unmarried pregnant girl needs more than prenatal care and arrangements for delivery, and her physician must know how to see that she has what she desperately needs. A personnel director may be aware that he would not have to fire a valued employee for insubordination if he could find someone to help the man solve his marital problems that are creating the tensions which make him lose his temper on the job. These and dozens of others have felt the need to know more about the kinds of muddles, financial, medical, emotional, into which mortals may entangle themselves, more about why they get into the muddles, and much more about the resources that exist for their aid.

In order to give help wisely one needs knowledge far beyond the scope of intuition and fine intentions. It is true that an ability to help others must start with sound common sense, an interest in what makes people behave as they do, and a sensitive reluctance to push square pegs into round holes. These qualities are basic, but something more is needed.

Let me draw a parallel. I can drive a car adequately because I have naturally quick reflexes and a good eye for clearances, and because I have learned by experience that if I do certain things with my hands and feet, certain results may be expected from the car. Moreover, I want to obey the traffic laws. This is all very well while the motor is running smoothly, but let something go wrong with the complicated mechanism of my car and I must needs sit helpless until someone more knowledgeable comes along. So it is with human relationships. Good intentions and alert common sense may be enough in dealing with the well-adjusted person; but a great many things can go wrong with the psychic as well as the physical mechanisms of a great many human beings, and the more there is wrong, the more there is need for specialized knowledge and trained skill to set things right.

A deal of damage can be done by the kindly, well-intentioned blunderer. Look at a few typical instances.

Perhaps a miserably unhappy girl asks for advice about the out-of-wedlock child she is carrying, and an overzealous friend urges marriage on moralistic grounds. Maybe this immature girl and the sullen boy can make a successful life together, but the chances are that they will be the worst possible mates for one another, and tragically inadequate parents for the unwanted child who will grow up in a neighborhood where uncharitable folk remember his beginnings.

Or perhaps a young wife, feeling imposed upon and misunderstood, goes to a girl friend who eagerly assures her that she should leave her husband and embark on a career. But in a week the newlyweds have reconciled their differences, and neither one speaks to the friend again. No great damage has been done in this situation —except to the confidante's vanity—but there might have been.

Or suppose an upright woman, shocked by the dirty housekeeping and unbalanced diet of a family across the tracks, exerts pressure to have the children removed from their home. Does this good woman really know whether these particular children will suffer more from the loss of the casual, warm love of their parents, or from the unwashed bed linen and the daily breakfasts of black coffee and jelly doughnuts? Applying one's own standards and one's

own ideals of a good life is not always the best way to help somebody else.

The possibility of errors in judgment is not confined to the non-
professional lay public. It can appear in the office of a welfare
agency, the very organization set up to help people in trouble. Here
are a few examples quoted by Hilary Leyendecker of situations that
demand far more than kind intent:

Sam Brown is barely literate; not only is he completely unskilled, but
he is clumsy and unreliable. Should he get a job, his employer will soon
find him a liability, and discharge him at the first opportunity. Suppose
that Sam makes no real effort to find work; suppose that he "likes to
lie a-bed of mornings"? Can we be sure that this is due to plain "cussed-
ness"? Could it not be that his not feeling like working might be the
result of poor nutrition, of rotting teeth, of bad eyesight, of a profound
but unrecognized discouragement?

Sarah Smith, ADC recipient, is the mother of four children all born
out of wedlock to different fathers—two since she began to receive public
assistance. If Sarah is in need, and if the men who fathered her children
cannot be located or are unable to provide support, should she be denied
assistance because of her behavior? Is the denial likely to impress upon
her the advantages of a virtuous life? Or is it likely to benefit the children?

Bill Jones has deserted his wife and three children and is living with
another woman by whom he has had three more children. For years Mr.
Jones supported both families; now he can support only one. Should
Mrs. Jones be denied assistance because it is her husband's responsibility
to support her and the children? Is this likely to prompt Mr. Jones to
return to the bosom of his legitimate family? If so, what will happen to
his other children? [1]

In situations such as these, one's first impulse is not necessarily
one's second. Should one try to save the public's money—and what
would be a saving in the long run? Should the offenders against
moral law be punished? And what of the innocent who must suffer
with the offenders?

Ella Lee Cowgill gives another instance:

[1] Hilary Leyendecker, *Problems and Policy in Public Assistance* (New York:
Harper, 1955), pp. 278 ff.

The worker, who was inexperienced, could not understand why John Standish was always late for his job in the factory and as a consequence was fired. She superficially saw Mr. Standish as a big strapping fellow who was too lazy to get up in the morning. When he applied for relief, the worker argued with him, taking the attitude that his present situation was entirely his fault.

Mr. Standish was used to having people take this fact for granted. His wife did, his boss did, his wife's mother did. He unconsciously looked upon all these people with hostility. Now this person from whom he must get a relief order or go home to a hungry and resentful family empty handed, was making the same assumption. He had long ago given up trying to explain his situation to anyone. No one would believe what he said anyway. Besides, how could he explain that his wife wept or argued far into the night and then objected when he wanted her to get up and get breakfast for him. She even complained that he disturbed her when he got up to get it for himself. The last person to whom he could explain his situation was this young woman before whom he was now sitting and who was telephoning his last place of employment about his work record. When the boss told her that "the only time he wasn't late was when he wasn't there" she had turned on him and said, "You lost your job for being late. What right have you to come here and ask for relief?" Instead of explaining, he got sullen and demanded an order saying that he would stay there until he got it. After all, as bad as this situation was, it was better than facing an angry wife and hungry family. The worker finally reluctantly gave him an order. Mr. Standish went out, vowing he would never come to that place again. He had formed his opinion of relief, of relief workers, and of his government, and in no sense was it complimentary. He classed them all as his enemies. He never did come back; instead, when the order was gone, he left home. The worker never knew what became of him but it is probable that he joined the ever increasing group of men wandering from city to city. As a result, the relief organization had a fatherless family to care for.[2]

The worker in this agency wanted to avoid unwise expenditure of public funds, but she succeeded only in putting a long-term relief case on the rolls. She wanted to persuade a man to assume his proper responsibilities, but she failed in that too. To quote Mr. Leyendecker's comment on this case:

[2] Ella Lee Cowgill, *A Guidebook for Beginners in Public Assistance* (New York: Family Service Association of America, 1940), p. 22. Quoted by Leyendecker, *op. cit.*, pp. 283 ff.

We see a man whose economic problems arose because of his inability to cope with a family problem. His wife appears to be a disturbed person, and his weakness is also not without significance. To establish himself economically, he needed not only immediate financial assistance but help with the situation that was causing this need. One of his needs, therefore, was to have someone try to understand the situation *as he saw it.* The fact that he did not express this need in so many words made it none the less real. He couldn't, in fact, discuss it until he had some assurance that the worker was capable of understanding him. She wasn't. . . . Had she been trained in human relations, she could have averted a broken home and a long-term dependency and saved the tax payer thousands of dollars.[3]

It would be possible to go on for pages describing situations which lure the well-intentioned into errors of judgment, situations in which the wise and most helpful move is by no means self-evident, situations in which the person in trouble does not know himself what is best, or does not say what he really means, or wants one thing today and another tomorrow, or cannot endure to face the unflattering realities of his own inadequacies and therefore makes a request based on a completely erroneous picture of his own capacities.

The skills and knowledge needed by anyone who hopes to give practical help or emotional support do not come by instinct and intuition. The worker must have a self-effacing technique for uncovering how a person feels about himself, his life, and the special predicament in which he finds himself. The worker must have knowledge of community resources that may be called on for aid. And it is imperative that he should have a control in using his own personality to provide a strengthened relationship, neither giving sympathy from his own hungry need to win response and gratitude nor witholding it because of a prejudiced impulse to punish weakness and ineptitude.

All of this takes more than kind intent.

However, it has not been easy for the layman to learn what he needs to know for better understanding of human relations and human motivations. Publications meant for graduates of schools of

[3] Leyendecker, *op. cit.,* p. 285.

social work present difficulties to the untrained. Look at the words they use: "Ambivalence," "empathy," "orthopsychiatry," "psychosomatic," "reactive disorders"! Even more familiar words such as "transference" and "identification" appear in strange company, obviously loaded with implications far different from those accepted by the uninitiated.

The very term "casework" sometimes frightens laymen, and it even leaves such professional people as doctors and teachers feeling uneasy. There still persists in the minds of some the misconception that casework has to do only with poverty, with investigations of "worthiness," with Thanksgiving baskets graciously bestowed by a Lady Bountiful. It is true that casework is a technique to be learned and used by those social agencies concerned with relieving financial need, but it is also a technique applicable in any of the helping professions. It is concerned with much more than the handing out of cash relief. Marital discord, delinquency, all sorts of behavior problems and personality upsets fall within the caseworker's ken, and one who would apply the casework techniques must know far more than whether the client is "deserving," a quality of the least possible interest to the truly helping person.

Mary Richmond's *Social Diagnosis,* published in 1917, stresses the importance of social relationships in developing personality, and the need for caseworkers to secure information which will give a clue to the basis for personality problems. At about this same time and in the years following, a number of books appeared in the related fields of sociology, psychiatry, psychology, medicine, and mental hygiene, all expressing with increasing emphasis and assurance the conviction that undesirable behavior is not the result of innate and incurable perversity, but is a response to urges and impulses conditioned by environment and by early experiences.

So this book is written, not for graduates of the schools of social work, but for caseworkers who have been plunged into their jobs without specialized training; for teachers and school nurses who need often to apply casework techniques in their day-by-day work; for doctors, lawyers, ministers, who not only use casework in their professional contacts but need to be aware of what social agencies, public and private, have to offer their clients. It is written, too, for the average citizen who would like to be of help to a troubled neighbor, but is a little uncertain how to proceed without damage to pride or intrusion of privacy.

This is not a brief on "How to be a Caseworker in Six Easy Lessons." The art of helping people cannot be learned in six lessons, or in sixty. This book is no more than an effort to explain in straightforward language what casework is, the kinds of information which are needed by a person who uses casework techniques, how he uses the information he has, where he can learn more of the skills he should have to avoid blundering in this delicate art of helping people.

However, neither information nor intelligence is sufficient, although both help. Nor is kind intent enough, although that too helps. The best kind of casework requires education in the field of social work; it needs a sensitive feeling for people and an urge to help them; it demands maturity of judgment; and always it is deepened and improved with experience. Only a small part of all this can be won by reading. Nevertheless, reading is a step in the right direction, and after the wish to help people, it is probably the first very important step.

Elizabeth Nicholds

Cleveland, Ohio
September 1, 1960

A primer of SOCIAL CASEWORK

CHAPTER I

When people need help

HELPING PEOPLE is a delicate business that demands skill to discover what is really needed, information about resources that will provide what is needed, and a method of approach that will not hurt or offend. In other words, a technique. Let us look at a few situations in which casework is applicable.

A man comes to a doctor's office looking angry and rebellious. He has been hurt on the job, he says. His thumb is smashed and he may never be able to work again, but the company doctor is prejudiced, he insists, and has refused to recommend him for compensation. The whole thing is the foreman's fault, anyway, always picking on him and making him nervous. Because he was trying to hurry his hand slipped, and his thumb is smashed. The doctor examines the thumb and finds it skinned but not crushed. He does what little is required, and suggests that the man apply to the employment bureau for another type of job. At the bureau, when the man's work record is checked it is learned that his performance is of poor quality and behind schedule. Subsequent medical and psychological tests reveal that the man has inferior coordination and is actually incapable of operating with any efficiency the machine at which he had been stationed. It did not take the employment bureau long to locate a different kind of job for him, one that did not involve using any machine. In two weeks, feeling successful at his new and simpler job, the man forgot his resentment of the foreman and the "prejudiced" company doctor. He also forgot his "crushed" thumb.

A child goes to the school nurse saying that she has a stomachache, but her description of the pain is vague and contradictory, and examination soon convinces the nurse that there is no stomachache at all. It may be the child is malingering to avoid a difficult school situation—this interpretation would occur to any experienced school nurse—but the youngster's wistful expression and the way she leans against the nurse's shoulder, plus what is known of her home life, leads to a realization that what she needs is neither medication nor a scolding, but a liberal dose of the warm affection and personal attention which a too busy mother does not give her at home. So the nurse gathers the child on her lap and cuddles her a while before sending her back to the classroom.

A frantic woman is sobbing to her priest. In broken English she tells him that the doctor has said her child has a spot on one lung and must go to a hospital. But to this woman, hospitals are places where people die, and spots on the lung mean "the consumption," and people always die of that. The priest calms the woman, phones the doctor for accurate information, and then can assure the weeping mother that the situation is not too serious. The child's condition is not bad, childhood tuberculosis is not usually fatal, there are fine resources for its cure, and probably in a very few months her child will be home again quite healthy. He tells her where the sanitarium is located and he talks about the children he knows who have been cured there.

A high school senior tells the guidance counselor that she wants to shift from the academic to the commercial course. It is not fair, she says, to ask her parents to spend money on college for her. Her mother is not well, and she, the daughter, should stay at home to take care of her father. The counselor suggests that they take a little time to consider the situation and gives her an appointment in the following week. Before the appointment the counselor learns that the student's grades are satisfactory. She calls on the parents and discovers that the mother is not ill; moreover, they can afford college for their daughter and want it for her. In the course of the next few weeks, the counselor sees the girl half a dozen times. During these interviews they talk about what college means to the girl, her previous experiences away from home, what she wants to do with her life. It develops that she has never been away, and all she wants is to stay close to her father, whom she adores. Finally, the girl burst out, "I guess I'm just scared to leave home. My mother isn't really sick. Maybe I just sort of hoped she would be, to give me an excuse. But Dad would be disappointed if I didn't go to college. I better go."

We have seen here four situations and four different types of helping technique. The worker in the employment bureau applied *manipulation of the environment*. The school nurse gave a *supportive relationship*. The priest supplied *clarification of the problem*. The guidance counselor most tactfully used *interpretation* in a delicate emotional situation.

In the manipulation of environment circumstances are so rearranged as to reduce stress for the client. In this technique something outside the client, something other than his mental or emotional attitude, is changed and brought to bear on his life so that he can be more comfortable and more productive. This technique covers a multitude of activities—finding improved housing or better employment, changing the school program for a slow child, locating vocational training opportunities for a handicapped person, obtaining medical care for the ill, securing home nursing for temporary invalids. Environmental manipulation includes introducing a child to a club leader who can give him an opportunity to socialize, or persuading a troublesome mother-in-law to allow a young couple to work through their marriage adjustments without interference. It includes all the activities which help make available to the client the resources, physical, medical, social, educational, which he needs and is able to use.

Unhappily, this common and valuable technique is sometimes misused. An inexperienced person may be tempted to rush around manipulating the environment too eagerly, unaware that he is leaving confused and resentful clients in his wake. He may push a man willy-nilly into a job where the pay is better, without seeing that the threat of increased responsibility or the demand for new skills may make an already insecure person miserable, rendering him quite unable to work at all. Or he might take a child out of his home because the housekeeping standards are deplorable without stopping to think that the child's relationship with his own family is warm and comforting and good, and that the child can survive sleeping without sheets and spending the day minus a morning bath far better than he can face the loss of emotional security.

It is always the client's true needs, not the worker's feelings, that should determine whether or not the environment needs changing. A client may be able to accept a situation, as, for example, poor housing, that the caseworker would find abominable. Sometimes an individual, especially an old person, is more comfortable in a dingy place with which he is familiar than he could ever be in a spot that is antiseptic but strange. That is not to say that a client should be left in poor housing conditions just because he has never had anything better. A person who hopes to help must find out how the client feels about his environment before he starts manipulating it.

Sometimes a situation which looks bad, and in fact *is* bad, cannot be corrected. Then, if manipulation of the environment is out of the question, the worker must select another technique. Since what cannot be cured must be endured, the client must be helped to find the strength to face whatever he has to face. The problem may be the death of someone who was a source of security, or it may be a physical handicap that cannot be alleviated, or it could be the need to adjust his life to the difficult personality of some member of his immediate family. Such problems are real, and they cannot be dissolved. Only the client's attitude can change and strengthen. Widows must learn to carry on their lives alone. A paralytic must adjust to his condition. A blind man must live in the dark, a deaf man in his silence. Often the families of neurotic persons have no choice but to endure their exasperating behavior.

Supportive relationship is the technique to be used in these situations, the giving of sympathy, understanding, and personal support, a deliberate giving of affection and interest which is more than a means of strengthening the therapy; it is often itself the therapy. That is what the school nurse was doing for the little girl whose mother was too busy to pay much attention to her. With an adult it would not so much be affection which the caseworker would give, but acceptance without criticism, unwonted advice, or unrealistic encouragement. These would provide the supportive relationship to carry the troubled one over a hump of discouragement.

The danger in the attempt to use supportive relationship as a helping technique is that it may be confused with the sort of reassurance and encouragement which is given out of the worker's own need to be accepted and liked, without sufficient awareness of the effect the relationship may have on the client. It is difficult for any kindhearted person to face another who is in trouble without offering some sort of verbal reassurance, especially if there is danger that practical help will be a long time coming or will be impossible. But empty encouragement, proffered when there is no reality basis for encouragement, can be completely devastating. To tell a client that everything is going to be all right when worker and client both know quite well that everything cannot possibly be all right is to build on shifting sands. No client can have trust in a caseworker who deceives him, even though the deception is prompted by pity and kindliness.

Moreover, sympathy at the wrong time can be damaging. An adult client who is naturally strong is certain to be resentful if his strength is not recognized, and will in all probability withdraw from a relationship he finds humiliating. A person who might enjoy dependence may be embarrassed to admit it, and he too may stay away from a caseworker who seems to encourage him in his weakness. Both clients are thus made inaccessible to further help. On the other hand, a client who is willing to let himself become dependent will not be strengthened by prolonged sympathy. He may all too easily come to lean on it, never learning to manage for himself. Such a dependent client is certain in time to make excessive demands that result in guilt on the part of the worker who cannot meet them, resentment on the part of the client who feels rejected, and no lasting help at all.

Verbal reassurance and sympathy should be given sparingly, with alert awareness of their effect on the client, and only when the reassurance has some basis in reality or when sympathy can help a potentially strong individual live through a temporary period of discouragement. A real supportive relationship as a helping technique goes far deeper than a facile expression of sympathy and superficial encouragement.

Often the relationship which provides the most support is one that offers the opportunity for a disturbed and upset person to express his less desirable feelings without fear of reproof. Although behavior must be controlled if one is to live comfortably in society, still, verbalization, permitted in certain situations without criticism implied or overt, can release tensions which have been costing the client a great deal of energy to maintain, even to the point of influencing behavior adversely. Most of us, at one time or another, have had the experience of "blowing our top" and thereafter settling down to behave ourselves. The explosion has been especially efficacious if we did not have to apologize or justify it afterward. The placid acceptance of such a blow-off is a part of supportive relationship casework.

Embarrassing impulses and unwelcome emotions will, if they are suppressed, certainly create tension and may lead to behavior one does not intend and sometimes cannot even explain. The classic example is the man who, forced to submit all day to an overbearing employer, goes home at night to snarl nastily at his inoffensive wife. In varying degrees we have all done something of the sort. But if we had an opportunity to express our resentment, without fear of consequences, to an impartial and objective third person, we might be less tempted to spill our pent-up emotions on someone we were in a position to hurt. In the helping process, the caseworker can be that impartial and objective third person. The caseworker can let a mother talk as bitterly as she needs about the endless dusting, dishes, and diapers without letting her feel that she is being criticized for any lack of devotion to her home and family. If she can talk freely to the caseworker perhaps she will not be so tense that she shouts at the children before she can control herself. The caseworker can let the young woman who is tied to a disagreeable, complaining, invalid mother tell how much she yearns to escape. In talking, perhaps the woman's tension is released so that she can go on patiently taking care of her mother.

A "supportive relationship" means listening to the client without criticism or blame. It means thinking of him as an individual, a special person with a unique problem in which the worker too is deeply interested. It means treading a precarious path between sympathy that encourages self-pity and censure that creates guilt, defensiveness, and suppression.

"Clarification of the problem," the third technique used at one time or another by all workers, means putting the facts of a situation clearly before the client in words he can understand and in terms he can grasp: Childhood tuberculosis is not often fatal; hospitalization does not mean death. There is a good chance of recovery if the recommended course is followed. Epilepsy is not always a permanently disabling disease. There are ways of controlling it, and this is what you must do. . . . You do not have to go to the poorhouse if you are old and without means of support. There is Old Age Assistance, and to know whether you are eligible, here is what we must find out. . . .

To be made clearly aware of facts and possibilities and conditions may relieve a client of emotional stress and open the way for manipulation of the environment or for the use of other techniques of help. However, clarification of the problem, like the other techniques, can be misunderstood and misused by the inept caseworker. It can all too easily be confused with the giving of advice. It requires an almost superhuman degree of self-control to refrain from giving advice when one sees some bumbling individual ruining his life: "You are a very foolish woman. You should let your child be hospitalized so that he can have proper care." However, unless force is used, this advice will have no effect on the distraught mother. Until the mother understands the facts about her child's illness and the function of the sanitarium, she will not willingly permit him to leave home.

The caseworker who gives advice usually does so on the basis of the way he thinks he would feel if he were in the client's situation. But this is not necessarily the way the client feels. Different people feel differently. One man who has lost his job may be angry; another may feel discouraged and resentful; another, panic-stricken at the thought of his hungry famliy; another, secretly relieved. What each client needs is not a sermon on what the caseworker thinks he ought to do next but a clear explanation of what he can do if he will, what other jobs are available, where he can apply, what sort of help may be forthcoming if he does not get any job at all and how long such help can continue. Then, with the facts before him the client can make his own decisions and plan his own life. The caseworker's responsibility is to make quite certain that the clarification has really clarified the situation for the client in terms he can grasp.

Closely related to the error of giving advice is another mistaken approach that sometimes tempts the overeager caseworker who thinks he is applying the delicate technique of interpretation. Interpretation involves bringing to the surface of the client's mind the real motivations that he is hiding under rationalization or some other common defense mechanism. But interpretation, to be effective, must always come from the client himself, not from the caseworker, and no amount of pseudo psychiatric talk from the caseworker will accomplish anything: "You are behaving like a bully just because you don't want people to know how scared you really are." "You're staying home from the party because you think maybe you won't be popular and you can't face it." "You say those mean things to your sister just because you're jealous of her." Perhaps all that is true, but whether it is or not, to make such statements is completely futile. Explaining a client to himself is never effective, even if he believes what is said. Intellectual understanding has little or no effect on behavior. The client must arrive independently at this kind of understanding so that the conviction comes to him from within himself. The caseworker can leave the way wide open, but he cannot coerce the client and expect any good to come of it.

Carl Rogers says of intellectualized interpretation,

it might be termed the attempt to change individual attitudes by means of explanation. In general, this approach grew out of a better understanding of human behavior. As clinical counselors learned to understand more adequately the factors which underlie behavior and the causes of specific behavior patterns, they tended to make more and more adequate diagnoses of individual situations. Then came the natural mistake of assuming that treatment was merely diagnosis in reverse, that all that was needed to help the individual was to explain to him the cause of his behavior. . . . There was a naïve faith that this intellectual explanation of the difficulty would result in changed attitudes and feelings.[1]

---

[1] Carl Rogers, *Counseling and Psychotherapy* (Boston and New York: Houghton Mifflin, 1942), p. 25.

This faith was not justified. Psychiatric interpretation of unconscious motivations can bring childhood conflicts into the framework of adult understanding and open the way for them to be resolved, but the interpretation must come from within the client. In the incident described early in this chapter, the guidance director may have recognized quite soon that the schoolgirl was in bondage to a too close attachment to her father, jealousy of her mother, and a fear of losing her position as the center of her father's affection. But the girl would have been horrified if such an explanation had been thrust at her immediately. She would have rejected it, clung more tenaciously than ever to her original rationalization, and probably she would have walked out of the director's office never to return. But the director did all that any director or counselor or caseworker could do. She provided a climate of acceptance, a freedom from all judgmental attitudes, and gave the girl time to come spontaneously to a realization of her own motivation. Then and only then could the girl abandon her rationalization and make a decision based on reality.

Overstreet says that the aim of psychotherapy is to create for the disturbed individual a situation suitable for the rediscovery of early forgotten suppressed experiences.

The atmosphere must be free from censoriousness and reproach, for these would make the client put self-defense ahead of self-discovery. It must be free likewise from any suggestion of what the therapist would like the patient to say or feel or do, for the impulse to please might all too easily lead to self-deception—to trumped-up emotions or to the despairing sense of being once more a failure.[2]

If the caseworker is not sufficiently disciplined to remain silent and receptive while the client gropes, if he attempts a premature or unskillful interpretation, either of two results may be expected, neither of them good. If the client knows the language of psychiatry he may recognize the terms and give an intellectual acceptance to the interpretation. But intellectualization never influences emotional attitudes and rarely influences behavior. Moreover, it may encourage an unhealthy self-absorption to the extent that profitable activity is

[2] Harry and Bonaro Overstreet, *The Mind Alive* (New York: W. W. Norton, 1954), p. 46.

blocked. Or an unwelcome and premature interpretation on the part of the worker may result in prompt rejection by the client of both interpretation and worker, and thus successful attempts at further relationship become utterly impossible.

Casework help, then, can be given through manipulation of the environment, supportive relationship, clarification of the problem, or interpretation. Any one of these techniques may be damaging if it is applied in the wrong situation, or if it is ineptly applied. Each can be tremendously helpful when skillfully used in the situation where it is needed. Each may be used singly; more often, two or more are used in combination. Any one of them is good in the right place, but not all of them are equally suitable in every situation, and use of any of the techniques can result in complete failure if the worker has blundered in his diagnosis of the problem or of the personality of his client. Just as the success of any medical treatment must depend on its suitability to the patient and to the ailment, so the success of any helping technique must depend on the accuracy and sensitivity with which the caseworker has been able to evaluate the client and his circumstances.

Whichever one of the possible techniques is considered to be applicable, casework must always be practical, nonjudgmental, understanding. It must be practical in the sense that it deals with people as they are and with situations as they actually exist. The solution it offers, if it offers one, must be free from wishful thinking, and it must be realistic in view of the client's family situation and social setting, his physical and intellectual limitations, his education and training, his emotional maturity or lack of it.

Casework must be nonjudgmental since judging is not helping. Help can be given and used only if the caseworker can accept the client as someone who is doing the best he can with what he has— even though what he has may be insufficient mental equipment, inadequate emotional stability, skill, or training, and he may have lacked opportunities as well.

Casework must be understanding since only if a caseworker knows how the client feels about his special situation can he determine what kind of help the client needs and can use.

It is worthy of note that not one of the "caseworkers" mentioned at the beginning of this chapter embarked on his plan of help before making a thorough study of the problem both from the point of view of the troubled "client" and also from that of other individuals involved: the foreman of the angry workman; the family of the love-hungry child; the priest who knew the child with tuberculosis; the parents of the high school student. The workers used, as each situation indicated, work history, medical reports, school records, family background—whatever was needed to provide complete understanding.

The next few chapters, therefore, will present a study of how a worker proceeds in securing the information that he needs to determine an accurate diagnosis of the situation and an understanding of the client's personality.

CHAPTER II

First steps in helping

IT IS SO CLEAR as to be almost self-evident that the first steps in helping must be to find out what the problem is, to learn what the client wants done about it, to uncover the resources both within the client's personality and in his environment which can be used to correct the situation. Some of these steps, however, are too often overlooked, and none is so simple as it might appear. When a person turns to a caseworker for help, it is imperative that the worker learn promptly what the external situation actually is and how much practical help, if any, is needed at once. If a man's house is burning down, one does not pause to inquire how the fire started, nor attempt at once to correct the man's lamentable habit of falling asleep with a lighted cigarette in his hand. When a man is in trouble, one's immediate interest is to learn the facts and do something quickly about the emergent situation. Then, and only then, does one undertake long-term planning.

It is true, however, that the facts of the situation may not be as the client presents them. For one thing, he may not have all the pertinent information—concerning his health, for example. Or he may be tempted to add a year or so to his age in order to qualify for Old Age Assistance, or suppress information which he fears may make him ineligible for the help he seeks or personally unacceptable to the caseworker. Whatever the reason that blocks the client from telling the truth, the whole truth, and nothing but the truth, it is quite evident that the person who hopes to help him must get at the facts, one way or another, complete and clear of error and misrepresentation.

This suggests that many statements made by the client at the first interview should be amplified or verified through other sources. Sometimes inexperienced workers feel a qualm lest they offend by indicating the need for verification. No offense should be taken. If the caseworker is neither apologetic nor defensive, if he takes it quietly for granted that matters must proceed in a businesslike way, the client will ordinarily accept the same point of view. Any loud or emotional objection to verification of his statements is itself significant. It may mean that the client has made a conscious effort to deceive, or it may mean that he is feeling humiliated by the need to ask for help and is reluctant to have others learn of his situation. Or there may be other explanations. In any event, his attitude indicates something important about his personality or his problem, and this is a matter for the caseworker to explore and understand.

First, then, what is the external situation? Following that, how does the client feel about it? What, if anything, has he already done to help himself? What more does he hope can be done for him? And what are his inner strengths and weaknesses that must be taken into account in the planning? What the client says and the way he says it suggest some of the answers, but we must go farther and probe deeper before we can be certain what manner of man our client may be. For one thing, his behavior at the moment of stress as he asks for help may not present an accurate picture of his overall personality. Hysteria when catastrophe falls unexpectedly, defensiveness assumed to cover embarrassment, may not reflect the client's true personality at all. The alert caseworker must maintain a nicely balanced combination of the accepting, interested manner which encourages a client to talk frankly and an objectivity which saves the worker from being swept off his feet by a client's urgency before the facts of the situation are clear. To carry our previous figure of speech a bit further, if the worker sees that his client's house is burning, he puts out the fire if he can; but before he plans to build another he finds out what kind of house the client thinks he would like, whether such a house is really suited to him and his family, whether he can maintain it, and possibly whether the current conflagration was started by some habitual act which has resulted in previous fires and may cause another. Some of all this the client

tells freely, or the caseworker gathers from direct observation; more
of it he must learn or confirm from other sources—the client's family, his neighbors, employer, pastor, doctor, or the firemen who
helped put out the fire and examined the ruins.

But it is high time to abandon our overworked analogy and get
back to a real client in a more probable situation. A man we will
say, comes to an agency to ask for help in finding employment, or
for cash assistance to carry him over a lean time between jobs, or
for advice on marital problems, or on how to manage his children
who are getting out of hand, or on any of the other numerous problems that baffle and plague unhappy mortals. The caseworker must
move with caution. What the man asks for may not be what he
needs or can use. He is too closely involved with his own problems
to see with any perspective, so perspective is what the worker must
supply and accuracy of information is what he must seek. The man
must not be sent off to a job in which he cannot possibly succeed.
Divorce must not be recommended until the wife too has been interviewed and the situation evaluated. The children must not be adjudged delinquents until much more is known about them than one
man can tell and that man an exasperated and worried father whose
impatience and exasperation may cause the bad behavior.

When a client asks for help, there are a number of things that
must be found out about him. A few of these the worker can see
for himself as the client walks into the office. Others will emerge as
the story is told. But many of these, including some which the
worker thinks he has observed himself, need confirmation or interpretation from other sources. The facts with which a worker should
be armed before he can make an accurate diagnosis fall readily
into two groups. First, there are those which are inherent in the
individual himself, such as his physical appearance, his mental
abilities, his special skills; and second, there are those which pertain
more to his environment, such as the type of house he lives in, the
sort of associates he enjoys, the kind of employment he has now or
has had in the past. The two groups are interrelated, affecting each
other, and both groups are important since the problem itself may
fall into either group, and since the facts to be obtained from either
group may affect the client's ability to use help.

The first group, those inherent in the person of the client, are all those physical factors which can strongly influence attitudes and can even at times make or break a personality. Some of these are evident at the first sight one has of a client—his general appearance, for instance. Has he average good looks, or is he outstandingly handsome or unusually plain? Either way, his personality may well be affected. Is he very tall or very short, fat or thin? Has he any obvious deformity or abnormality? Even minor departures from the norm that should not be important to a well-balanced person can be pretty devastating to someone who feels none too secure at best. Crooked or protruding teeth, acne, overlarge ears, can be crushing matters to an adolescent and even to some adults. People who are overweight are notoriously sensitive about it, and so are unusually tall persons, especially tall girls. Undersized men are equally affected. Physical handicaps can seriously undermine confidence, although some persons with a strong ego development will over-compensate and appear more confident because of the handicap. Very small men, for example, sometimes appear to strut.

Such points can be observed during the initial interview although how the client feels about himself may not be so immediately apparent. It must be remembered that it is how the *client* feels that is important, not how the worker thinks he might feel in the client's shoes. Red hair may be the bane of a child's existence although to an adult it appears strikingly attractive. Obesity may be repugnant to a style-conscious agency worker, while to a woman from another level of society it may seem comfortable and quite acceptable. If the woman's husband likes his wife to be "a tidy armful" the case-worker should not worry about her. Watch for the client's reaction to the physical aspects observed, remembering always that the client may not be willing or able to verbalize his reaction. Perhaps the client's inner feeling can be discovered only through discussion with a collateral source, such as his doctor, a teacher, another member of the family.

There are other physical factors not so apparent which are equally important in an evaluation of a client's potential, factors whose existence can be learned only through medical reports. Glandular imbalances, for example, histories of long illnesses, old injuries, accidents, and operations, all may be highly significant. Also important are the special skills or aptitudes of the client, both for the way in which they may influence the client's attitude toward himself and for the possibilities they open for future planning. The smooth coordination of an athlete, or a good singing voice, or the ability to use the hands in small and accurate manipulations, may open the way to improved employment or to a therapeutic hobby. But these characteristics must be verified through sources other than the client's statement, if, indeed, he makes any statement whatever on the subject.

Among the environmental factors, quite possibly the most significant are those of the home situation. If the client happens to be a child, it is clearly important to have accurate information about the parents. The attitude of parents toward each other and toward their child create an atmosphere in the home that either helps or hinders the process of growing up. Both neglect and overprotection may distort a child's personality. The educational standards and mental abilities of the parents will probably indicate the amount of intellectual stimulation the home is offering. For an adult client, it is important to know something about the marital relationship, the number and ages of the children, the extent of family responsibilities. Sometimes it is helpful to know the kind of home in which the client grew up, since early background will carry its influence into adulthood and many of the personality problems of the grown man can be understood only in the light of his childhood experiences.

The wider circle of community standards is equally worth study. The social, moral, and educational expectations of the neighborhood in which the family lives have a strong influence on what the individual comes to expect of himself. An income may be adequate in one setting but quite inadequate to maintain the social standards which a man at another address has set for himself. Employment which provides a sense of status in some communities may be regarded with scorn in another, and if a man's work leaves him feeling embarrassed and defensive, there is sure to be tension which operates adversely on emotional adjustment and on behavior.

Another factor that may well be of immense importance to a

man's personality is the religious. Caseworkers in public agencies and workers connected with nonsectarian organizations are often taught to avoid the controversial subject of religion. But if religion is a strong influence in a client's life, that is a fact to be remembered in diagnosing the potential and in planning the help.

Quite obviously, not all these factors are of equal importance in all situations. An adolescent's embarrassment over acne may affect her social poise and even her academic attainments, but it has no part in her emergent need if her leg has been broken in an auto accident. A man's childhood conflicts may influence his marital adjustments but not his business success or lack of it. Or they may enter both areas. The caseworker must be forever alert to the possibility of a factor entering a client's thinking or his unconscious attitude even though that factor seems to the worker quite foreign to the immediate situation. Some religious sects object to blood transfusion; others, to employment on Saturday. Racial habits of diet, neighborhood attitudes toward premarital sex experience, the variation in feeling in different geographical areas toward race segregation—any one of these may or may not be significant in planning with a client. But the caseworker must remember to keep the possibility of their importance well in mind.

The moral of this whole chapter is that we must know the facts of a situation before we plan, and that many statements must be verified rather than accepted at face value when they come from a person who by the nature of things must be prejudiced. Even the caseworker's own guesses and conclusions arrived at from early observation should be confirmed and interpreted before a plan is based on them. This is true for psychological as well as social, financial, and physical data. A caseworker in a public agency is not likely to question the necessity for verification of financial need through a check of bank balances or property resources. Birth dates are verified if a client applies for Old Age Assistance; degree of blindness or of disability would be confirmed by medical reports if the application were for Aid to the Blind or to the Disabled. But we must be equally certain of our facts in less tangible areas. A client who says he is having difficulty with his boss may be projecting his own insecurity, in which case he would very likely have similar difficulties with any boss on any job. On the other hand, the difficulties may be quite realistic, due to a verifiable inefficiency on the part of the client, or a verifiable orneriness on the part of the boss, in which case the client needs a different job or a different boss. The case-worker could be certain of the diagnosis—and the plan—only by interviewing the boss, or by studying the client's previous work record, or by talking to a few of his fellow workers. A client may assert that religion is a strong motivating force in his life. This may be true, or the client may be saying what he thinks might impress the worker, or he may be describing an imaginary portrait of himself developed through wishful thinking because years ago that is the image his mother taught him was admirable. Only an interview with his pastor or with members of the man's family could determine which is the true picture.

So we turn now to the technique of interviewing, that basic tool by which any caseworker arrives at his diagnosis—interviews with the client himself, or interviews with someone else in his behalf.

CHAPTER III

Techniques of interviewing

MUCH of the information on which a caseworker is to base his plan for the client must of necessity come through the personal interviews which he has either with the client or with someone who is in a position to tell him about the client. Indeed, a large proportion of the help itself is effected through face-to-face conversation. Interviewing is such an important tool for anyone who hopes to help people in trouble that facility in the use of it should be learned as a pianist learns his scales or a singer, breath control. Although sensitivity is vital for successful interviewing (just as a feeling for music is important to musicians), still, practice improves technique, and observance of some of the rules brings success more easily.

In any interview, the setting can help or it can hinder. Sometimes, of course, there is no opportunity to select the setting, and the worker must conduct the interview where he finds it. Circumstances may indicate that it must take place in the interviewee's home, with the television going full blast, children running in and out, neighbors kibitzing, and mother worrying about what is cooking on the stove. If the setting is very unsuitable, it may be the better part of valor to retreat until another time or another place can be arranged; but if postponement is impracticable, then one does the best one can. One may offer to wait until the kitchen crisis is over. The television can be shut off by a twist of the wrist. But there is no button to press that will stop the children's racket, and in another person's home it is difficult to do much about the unwelcome presence of neighbors without giving offense.

Callers, or even other members of the family, can create a real problem. Anyone reacts in some degree to an audience, even if it is only with increased reticence. Mother may not want to talk freely about Junior's behavior in front of that gossiping old hen from next door, and Father may not want to appear to his mother-in-law as someone who can be pushed around by a social worker. All of this must be considered when the interviewer evaluates the interview. What has been said may not be quite what would have been said, nor all that could have been said, under other circumstances.

The more persons there are present, the more complicated the conflicting influences, and the more befogged the evaluation. The wise interviewer will therefore arrange for privacy if he can. Even if the interview cannot be held in a setting of his choosing, even if it must be in the interviewee's home, there are a few steps the worker can take to secure privacy. He might suggest that the mother, or whoever is the chief interviewee, should sit in the interviewer's car to talk. Or he could ask that they move from the crowded living room where the children are watching television into the kitchen, where there is a table on which he can write.

There are, of course, exceptions to the general desirability of privacy. A counselor studying a child's behavior will probably want at least one interview in which he can observe the child and his parents together so that he can see the interplay between them. If a couple is applying at an adoption agency for a baby, it is desirable to see husband and wife at the same time in order to get a picture of their relationship. Sometimes, even though the interviewer would a little rather talk to a person alone, it may nevertheless be better to see him in his own environment, taking a chance on privacy, rather than force him into the unfamiliar setting of an office where he may be stiff and uneasy.

If the interview is to take place in the worker's office it should be possible to control at least the physical aspects of the setting. The atmosphere should be relaxed, physically comfortable, and free from distracting noise. If the interviewee is a very junior person it might be wise for the worker tactfully to make certain that the child does not want to go to the bathroom, and that there is a supply of tissues handy in case of the sniffles. One appointment failed completely of its purpose because the interviewee, aged nine, needed to blow her nose, and the interviewer was not sufficiently intuitive of a small girl's embarrassment to offer a handkerchief.

There should be no interruptions during the interview and there should be no unnecessary prior delay in the reception room. Any long preliminary wait will increase tension, either of resentment or apprehension, and interruptions or distracting noises break the train of thought equally for interviewer and for client. If either interruption or delay is unavoidable, then the worker should minimize their effect as much as possible by apologizing and making it quite clear that he is as much bothered as the interviewee.

Since the purpose of any helping interview is either to secure information needed to help the client, or to make it possible for the client to explain himself and his problem and his feelings, it is important that he should be put at ease as quickly as possible. The atmosphere of the interview should be one of relaxation with no pressure of haste, and the attitude of the interviewer should be one of interest, attention, and helpfulness. It should be the worker's first objective to feel out the interviewee's state of mind, and take that as his starting point. If the client has come voluntarily to a familiar agency to ask for a specific type of help which he has received on previous occasions from this agency, that is one thing; it is quite another if he is coming for the first time to a strange agency, not at all sure he is in the right place, or that he will not find the door closed in his face. It is still another if a reluctant client has been referred by some higher authority and comes with resentment, with shame, with apprehension, possibly with no recognition at all that he has any problem with which this unfamiliar interviewer could help. Imagine the contrast between the attitude of a man who has repeatedly received home relief during intervals between his seasonal employment and the attitude of a proud old man who has been self-supporting all his life but has outlived his ability to work and comes now to apply for Old Age Assistance, not quite sure what this type of assistance is, nor whether he is eligible, nor what demands may be made of him before he can receive it. And both would be different from the attitude of a man who has been adjudged by the Children's Court as neglecting his children and is sent by the judge to discuss plans with a child welfare agency for placement of his children away from home.

All these factors a worker must understand, since the interview must always be adapted to the client, emotionally and intellectually. Is he shy and ill at ease in an unfamiliar setting? Just because the interviewer is so accustomed to his own office he may forget what it can look like to a stranger coming in for the first time on an errand about which he may be acutely unhappy. How does the client feel about his reason for coming to the interview? Is he antagonistic because of fear and guilt, like a bad boy sent to the principal's office for punishment? Maybe he needs a little time to pull himself together in this strange, uneasy setting. If so, the interviewer may talk brightly for a while about the weather or some other impersonal topic. Perhaps the interviewee needs some explanation about the function of the agency—not too much, however, until the worker knows why he has come and what makes him feel the way he does. But it is possible that both insecurity and resentment may come from misunderstanding. The interviewer must not assume that the client is acquainted with the agency's function because he himself is so aware of it. Perhaps he should make these things clear to the client, or perhaps what is confusing the client is uncertainty as to the eligibility requirement for the type of assistance he hopes to receive. Or perhaps he is still thinking of social agencies as instruments of punishment.

Whatever the client's mood, that must establish the key in which the interview opens. If he is nervous or resentful, the worker must try to establish an easier relationship before going on to the intimate matters. If, on the other hand, the client is bursting to pour out his troubles, probably the interviewer should let him talk freely even if they must go back later for important background material. Always any interview must start where the client is and move ahead only as fast as the client can move.

If the interview is chiefly for the purpose of learning facts rather than opinions or attitudes the interviewer need not be afraid to take ample notes and may even ask the client to spell names and repeat dates in order to assure accuracy. New caseworkers are frequently bashful about note-taking in front of an interviewee, but notes are usually expected in this type of interview and in fact are often regarded by the client as proof of the importance of what is being said. A client applying for home relief once stopped in mid-flight to demand of the caseworker, "Ain't you going to put that down?" Rogers, in *Counseling and Psychotherapy*,[1] tells of taking down on the tape recorder interviews that touch on quite intimate material. The recording is always done with the client's knowledge and consent, and has never seemed to hamper an interview in any way.

On the other hand, absorption in note-taking should never be permitted to leave the client feeling that he does not have the whole attention of the interviewer. The worker should look as much as possible directly at the interviewee, and his expression should be one of alert listening. It is possible that tape-recording is better than note-taking, not only for its accuracy and its ability to catch nuances of vocal expression, but also in that it permits the worker to give undivided attention to the interviewee. One client once stormed out of an office outraged because "that fool girl never looked at me once, just sat making squiggles in her notebook!" As in all else, a nice balance is required.

If a client cannot seem to talk freely at the outset of the interview, the caseworker can help by asking superficial questions about unimportant matters to give him time to pull himself together— questions about his trip to the office, for instance, or the ubiquitous weather. If that tactic does not break through the self-consciousness and reserve, the questions may creep closer and closer to intimate matters until they touch on the subject of real concern. If the interviewer does not have advance notice of the client's reason for coming in, and if the client cannot express his need voluntarily, the worker may have to do quite a bit of fishing before he brings up something important.[2]

If the client is not so much embarrassed as he is sulky or resentful, the caseworker's questions should be of the sort that cannot be

[1] Rogers, *Counseling and Psychotherapy*, pp. 261 ff.
[2] An excellent example of this type of difficulty and the manner in which it can be met is quoted in Annette Garrett, *Interviewing: Its Principles and Methods* (New York: Family Service Association of America, 1942), Chap. XIV.

answered by a simple "yes" or "no." Once the interviewee has begun to talk in complete phrases about anything at all, he may progress to talking about important matters.

Sometimes silence is a useful tool, and the interviewer should not be afraid to make use of it. Most people are made uneasy by silence and will plunge in with any sort of verbiage to bridge an embarrassing pause. If the interview has begun at all, and is showing signs of moving in the desired direction, then silence from the interviewer may be a most valuable technique. If a worker can discipline himself to be quiet and relaxed, obviously receptive, it is very possible that the pause will build up until the dam breaks and the client pours out the feelings that he has been suppressing. This, however, is an effective technique only after the interview has made a start. Used too early, before a good relationship has been established, silence may only succeed in making a wrathful client stamp out of the room.

If the client is resentful at being forced into an interview—if a child, for instance, has been sent to a guidance center by the school or by his baffled parents—then the interviewer will have to talk easily and superficially long enough to convey his amiable intentions. However, sooner or later the interviewer should give this type of reluctant client an opportunity to express resentment openly. Perhaps the worker might even express it for him: "I expect you're not very happy about coming here, are you?" Once the resentment has been freed, the client may be able to talk about whatever is back of the feeling.[3]

In fact, the client should be given every opportunity to release in talk tensions of any kind if that is what he seems to need, even if the interviewer has already grasped the problem and is in a hurry to move on toward a concrete plan of help, and even if the whole tale is an old and familiar one. Red Cross workers in a disaster area are obliged to listen to the same story over and over again from different families who have been burned out or flooded out. To the worker, the story is the same each time. To the victim, it is all new and

---

[3] Rogers, *op. cit.*, p. 69, quotes a difficult interview with a child who was reluctant to talk openly, and did so only after the counselor had given her an opportunity to express her resentment.

personal and terrifying and pressing for release in talk. One of the worst errors any worker can make is to let a client feel that he knows the whole story before the client has a chance to tell it.

If the client has been referred by one agency to another, it is probable that some sort of case summary has preceded him to the second agency and is reposing in the desk drawer at the very moment that the second caseworker is holding the interview. But the client should be allowed to talk if he wants to. It is possible, of course, that he may not want to go over his story again in every detail, especially if it concerns trouble of long standing that he has reviewed until he is sick of it and hopeless. But the chances are that he will want to express his point of view and he should be allowed to do so, even if to the new worker it seems a waste of time. The repetition may not bring out new facts, but it helps, nevertheless, to give the client a feeling that this new caseworker is interested in him as an individual.

The relationship between the worker and the client is of utmost importance in any interview, and in any helping situation. The person who hopes to help must never forget that his own manner is affecting the client for better or for worse. An inexperienced interviewer may be shy or insecure or unsure of himself or afraid that he will not remember what is said or that he will not think of all the questions he should ask; or he may be belligerent to cover his own uncertainty; or nervous if he expects pugnacity from the client; or defiant because he has made up his mind in advance that he will probably meet resistance. Or he may be critical or judgmental; or too quickly reassuring and sympathetic. Any of these attitudes is sure to affect the client, possibly making it difficult for him to unload his troubles freely, or rendering him uncertain that he will get any help if he does. Then he will be tense or mute with discouragement; or belligerent in response to the interviewer's belligerence; or he may overemphasize his tribulations for the sake of leaning on sympathy from a softhearted listener; or he may exaggerate the drama of his situation because that seems the way to win attention. Whatever the interviewer's attitude, it is certain to influence the client in one way or another, and this must be taken into consideration when the results of the interview are evaluated.

An interviewer must never forget the impact his own personality and appearance may be having on the client, even in small ways and quite possibly in ways which the interviewer cannot possibly foresee. Maybe a caseworker looks like the client's stern grandfather and the client is feeling the way he did when he was caught smoking cornsilk behind the barn. Or maybe a lady caseworker looks a little like his mother, and he is beginning to want to bawl on her shoulder and be comforted as his mother once comforted him. These are effects the interviewer cannot anticipate and may have difficulty in identifying during the interview, but all caseworkers must be alert for them. It may be desirable to counteract the attitude of the client, or it may be possible to make use of it, but either way the case-worker must first become aware of it.

Nor must the caseworker forget the importance of small personal details that may have an unexpected effect on the client and on the success or failure of the interview. Little mannerisms, for in-stance, may have a most unfortunate effect, creating tension in the interview. Mannerisms such as nail biting, swinging a crossed foot, rhythmically tapping a pencil, snapping a ball-point pen, doodling, finger fidgeting, may be distressing and nerve-racking to an inter-viewee who is already strung pretty taut.

Psychiatrists and psychologists are trained to keep out of sight during analysis and while giving mental tests or to sit motionless so as to make themselves as inconspicuous as possible. A person who wants to help in the way caseworkers help people in trouble need not go that far—in fact he should not, since the skillful use of his own personality is a valuable part of the helping process. But he should not intrude disturbing aspects of his personality.

There are a few concrete suggestions that an interviewer would do well to remember as he evaluates the effect that his personality and his manner have on the client.

He should keep his voice down. People react to tonal pitch, often without knowing that they do. (This is true even with animals. A good animal trainer uses a voice low in pitch.) If the interviewer sounds excited, the client is likely to become tense and excited too, and, contrariwise, if the interviewer's voice remains controlled and quiet, the client's initial excitement may vanish.

The interviewer should speak slowly. Rapid-fire speech may rattle a slow thinker.

He should never finish a client's sentences for him even if the client seems to be groping for words. He may be a deliberate thinker who will give up trying if he is hurried, or if the worker says for him what he imagines the client has in mind. The worker may guess wrong, but the client may let it pass from diffidence or from a wish to find approval by doing and saying what seems to be expected.

No interviewer should allow himself to look bored or impatient. A client may continue talking into the lunch hour, but no one will starve.

If in the course of a worker's busy day it becomes imperative to end a rambling or repetitive interview, it must be done as courteously as possible: "Thank you for coming in. I'm glad to talk to you, but you must excuse me now. Someone else is waiting." There is always danger that even the gentlest termination will be interpreted by the client as a rejection, making it that much more difficult to establish sympathetic contact next time. But if it must be done, be honest and courteous.

Always end an interview with a clear indication of what is to happen next. Another appointment? More information to be secured by the worker from another source, with a subsequent appointment to be arranged with the client? Or is the client to bring additional information to the next interview? Whatever is to be done next, the interviewer must be explicit, remembering that the client is quite possibly too much upset to listen properly, unable to take in what is said. Certainly he will be less accustomed than the interviewer to agency routines. He will need exact explanations, often repeated, of what is to come next, and when, and where, and who, and how.

First, last, and always—all interviewers should remember the golden rule of interviewing: STOP—LOOK—LISTEN.

CHAPTER IV

The collateral interview

THERE ARE, in general, two types of interviews: the direct diagnostic, in which the client and the person who is to help him are face to face; and the collateral, in which the worker talks with a third person about the client who is to be helped.

A collateral interview may be instigated by an interviewee who is asking for help for another person. A teacher may come to a guidance clinic about a child whose behavior she finds unendurable. A man may come to a welfare agency about a dependent relative for whom he can no longer care. A neighbor wants to report an aging person who lives alone, needs assistance, but is too proud or too ill to come himself to the agency. In such situations the person making the referral is quite certain to come to his appointment prepared to give information and to answer questions about another individual. All that the interviewer needs to do is ask the right questions and explain what his agency can or cannot do for the one to be referred. If the agency can do nothing, or cannot do enough, the interviewer must explain why and suggest another resource. Handling an interview of this type does not demand interviewing skill so much as a clearheaded awareness of the scope of the agency and information about other community resources to which the interviewee may turn if the first organization is not equipped to give the help that is needed.

It sometimes happens that a "collateral" interview develops into a direct interview. A worried mother, for instance, comes to a psychiatrist to talk about the behavior problems of her child, and then makes it increasingly evident that her own personality problems are at the root of the matter, or her strained relations with her husband, or some other factor that might make her instead of her child the client. More skill is required to handle such a situation than is needed in the purely collateral interview, since usually an individual should not be encouraged to become too deeply involved in self-revelation if the agency to which he has come is not the one that can help him. On the other hand, the worker must learn enough about the problem to know where the interviewee should be referred. Or possibly the catharsis is badly needed by the interviewee at just this time, and to be stopped or referred elsewhere would be seriously damaging. But the problems peculiar to direct diagnostic interviewing will be faced in another chapter. Just now let us stay with the true collateral interview.

If the collateral interviewee has sought out the agency, and if the interview remains collateral, the problems are not likely to be complicated. Questions are asked and answered, an appointment is made for the worker to meet the client, or a referral is made to another agency better equipped to give the particular help required. But not all collateral interviews are simple ones. Perhaps the interviewer initiates the interview because he needs additional facts about a client already known to his agency. These interviews have been known to run into heavy weather.

An interviewer's first and toughest problem is to win the coöperation of the collateral, who may be indifferent, suspicious, or even downright antagonistic. An attendance officer calls on the parents of a truant, a probation officer wants to discuss with a defensive mother the problems of a predelinquent son, a caseworker from a public assistance agency hopes to get help for an old woman from her daughter who would much rather spend her income on herself—the situations are varied and the personalities involved so diverse that it would be almost impossible to offer rules that could be applied to all. Here are a few suggestions, however, that may be helpful.

The interviewer should hide as thoroughly as possible any tensions or doubts or nervousness that he himself may feel; for any visible tension will certainly communicate itself to the interviewee and create additional, responsive tension in him.

Arrangements should be made to hold the interview indoors if possible, but if an antagonistic interviewee stands foursquare in the doorway and does not invite the worker to come inside, he can only make the best of it and talk on the doorstep. However, sometimes simply taking for granted that he is to be asked in will be enough to get the worker inside. If it does not, the interviewer must not show irritation—in fact, he must not even be irritated. Perhaps the housewife is embarrassed about breakfast dishes still unwashed, or beds unmade. Maybe her inhospitality stems from a consciousness of some illicit goings-on indoors that are none of the worker's business and have nothing to do with the purpose of the call. If the interviewer suspects that to be the case, and if the possible goings-on are truly not his business, perhaps he can postpone the interview to a more favorable time.

If the worker gets inside but is not invited to sit down, that omission may indicate resentment of his presence, but it equally may indicate gaucherie on the part of the interviewee, and an insufficient training in manners, which has nothing whatever to do with her feelings toward the caseworker or the subject of the interview. In either case, the question, "Do you mind if we sit down?" will undoubtedly relieve the situation and make it easier to relax. It is usually better for both parties of an interview to be seated. If one sits while the other stands, there is an atmosphere of authority created which is not conducive to comfortable person-to-person contact. If both stand, haste is suggested. But an interviewer must be prepared to make the best of whatever situation he finds.

As soon as possible the interviewer should explain the purpose of the interview and his relationship to it. Sometimes an antagonism has developed wholly out of a misunderstanding of one or another of the items. The defensive mother of a predelinquent child, for example, may not know the function of a probation officer and may think her son is about to be dragged off to jail.

The caseworker should be courteous, and be prepared to show some degree of interest in the personal problems of the one to whom he is talking even though his main interest is to discuss the problems of somebody else. This does not mean that he should allow himself to become involved in long, intimate revelations about which he is prepared to do nothing, but maybe the interviewee is so tied up in knots because of his own frustrations that he cannot put his mind on anything else. Possibly the worker can get what he needs only by letting the interviewee unwind a bit.

At the same time, be realistic. If the schedule indicates that the worker must make ten widely separated calls a day, he cannot spend too much time in any one of them. He must keep control of the interview, finding a middle path between the projectile type that smashes through the interviewee's prejudices, curiosity, and sensitivity, and the meandering sort that moves in leisurely circles and never arrives anywhere.

Never be in too much of a hurry to allow the interviewee to tell his side of the story. Maybe the parent of the truant has what he considers an adequate reason for allowing the youngster to stay out of school. Or perhaps the daughter who will not support her indigent mother has financial worries of her own, a sick husband, an overwhelming debt. It always pays to learn the other fellow's point of view.

The interviewer should explain his relationship to the purpose of the interview. In some situations that may mean mentioning his title and position in the agency, even, perhaps, making clear his qualifications for undertaking the interview. He may find himself involved in an explanation of the aims and function of his agency. If so, he should keep it simple and brief so that it will not become confusing.

He may have to repeat questions asked by a previous visitor, or, if the interview is held in the worker's office, he may repeat questions asked at the reception desk. If so, he should explain why the repetition is necessary, for clients and collaterals alike usually resent a request to go over a story twice. Of course, there may be pent-up emotion that finds release in telling a dramatic incident over and over, but that does not usually apply to the giving of factual and statistical information. If an interviewee must be asked to repeat such material, he should be told why.

If possible, the interviewer should make certain in advance just what information is needed, and have all his questions well in mind so that a return trip will not be required. If, for instance, a school nurse visits the home of a child, she should be sure to have all the facts she needs to talk intelligently about the child and to ask the right questions—his grade in school, his attendance record, his behavior in the classroom, his school performance.

If the caseworker fills out a questionnaire in the course of an interview, he should be sure that he himself understands the purpose of each question and can explain it to the interviewee.

Questions should be asked in logical order if possible, so that one leads naturally into the next.

Be flexible. If the interviewee brings up a point that comes further along in the list of questions, the worker should follow his lead, and come back later to the bit that has been skipped.

Never forget that the interviewee is an individual, a personality in his own right. He may be one of several hundred whom the worker interviews, but to himself he is unique, and quite possibly the caseworker is the only interviewer with whom he talks. He may expect the worker to remember each detail of the interview he had a month ago, and the interviewer may have to go through some mental gymnastics to avoid letting him see that he has forgotten some points. But it is worth the effort.

Always end an interview on a practical, matter-of-fact note. If the atmosphere has been emotional, some trivial and superficial questions should be asked at the end. Or, if that is not practicable, talk for a minute about the weather, or any other impersonal subject. But do not leave an interviewee feeling upset. Give him an opportunity to pull himself together. (This exhortation ignores the horrid possibility that the worker never got beyond the point of the interviewee's initial anger. If a worker has to retreat in disorder while the interviewee shouts invective after him, the episode can hardly be termed an interview.)

Usually it is tactful to close an interview with some indication of the use to which the information will be put. If worker and interviewee are both interested in the client—a teacher, for example, and the interviewee the mother of a student—give, if possible, some indication of what is going to happen next. Maybe all that is going to happen next is another interview with another collateral about the same client, but if that is the case, it is tactful and courteous to say so. An individual can be justifiably annoyed if he answers a lot of questions but never finds out the end of the story.

CHAPTER V

The diagnostic interview

IT IS NOT for a moment to be forgotten that the techniques outlined in the last two chapters are only techniques, and of just about the same importance as fingering technique would be in the performance of a piano concerto. Without technique there will be blunders and false notes, but with *only* technique there will be no true music. There must also be feeling, if one is to create either music or human relationships. This is sufficiently true in any contact between person and person. It is doubly true in the direct contact between the person who wants to help and the one who is to be helped. A direct, face-to-face interview between these two should afford the caseworker not only the opportunity to learn at least some of the external facts of the client's situation, but also, and far more important, it should offer a chance to discover how the client himself is reacting to his situation, what his feelings are about himself and his predicament, what his strengths are, what his habitual pattern of behavior. Such a diagnostic interview, to be successful and productive, demands skill in techniques, it requires long practice, and most especially it needs a sincere feeling for the other person, an empathy for that person, an ability to relate to him, not as a typical case history, but as a separate and special individual with a unique problem and a unique way of responding to it.

Problems which some individuals can take in their stride will leave others overwhelmed and defeated. Blindness, striking a grown man, may be such a crushing blow that the victim is utterly unable to conceive a life for himself with any meaning until he has been given a great deal of emotional support. Perhaps he will never be able to accept his lot. Another man, with a stronger ego development, or perhaps with different skills and interests, may be able to think in terms of a useful future for himself and will need help only in vocational training. Or, to take another example, an unmarried mother may have lost all self-confidence because the father of the baby is no longer interested in her; or her mind may be wholly on the social implications of her situation; or she may forget her baby and herself in her strong urge to punish at all costs the man who has humiliated her by leaving her. No two individuals react in exactly the same way even to situations that appear on the surface to be identical. How a client feels about his circumstances and what he thinks he wants done about them should be revealed in the direct diagnostic interview between the client and the person who is to help. The whole picture will probably not emerge in one interview, but pieces will be added bit by bit in interview after interview until the picture is complete.

Another highly important function of the direct interview will be the establishing of a personal relationship between client and worker, a relationship which is often the foundation on which all help is based. It may even *be* the help. There will be more in another chapter about the use of this personal relationship, but here we will discuss more of the details of the technique which can, if the feeling is right, provide the diagnosis on which understanding is built of the person, his problem, and what can be done for him.

People are not always able to face their own emotional needs, or reveal them to another person. They rationalize their motives, they project their emotions onto someone else, they shrink from admitting to themselves or to anyone else the existence of embarrassing urges. They try in a dozen ways to hide their heads in the sand. Consequently, what they say they want is by no means always what they really want, or what they are able to use. The person who hopes to help must listen to the client explain himself, and as he listens, he must quietly make his diagnosis. Although he must know the facts of the external situation in order to know the area of stress, and although he must know how the client thinks he feels about his situation, the worker must also become acquainted with the client's customary behavior pattern so that he can foresee how any help which is offered is likely to be used.

One of the first questions to which an answer must be found is the extent of the stress under which the client is laboring at the moment. The interviewer can make an immediate and fairly accurate appraisal by observing the client's manner as he walks into the room and starts talking. Is his posture stiff and self-conscious? Are his gestures nervous? Is his voice strained? Does he talk too fast, with the overingratiating manner of one anxious to please? Such observations can provide a clue, but they must not be accepted as a final diagnosis until they are viewed in relation to the client's everyday attitude as seen in subsequent interviews or as reported by people who have seen him when he is not under stress. If the client's manner always suggests insecurity and tension, then that quality must be taken into account in assessing his character potential. If the manner is one peculiar to this interview, then the interviewer must consider the circumstances and what they mean to the client.

Leontine Young remarks:

The data acquired from all observations have to be screened twice: first, in relation to the situation in which they occurred, and, second, to check them with the normal reactions. . . . A prospective adoptive couple came to an agency to ask for a child. They were nervous, tense, and anxious. Their comments seemed cautious, perhaps placating, or even secretive. Unless the caseworker took into account that such an interview was anxiety provoking and created for the couple an abnormal situation, he could receive a totally false impression. The two people in this instance were responding quite normally according to their patterns, to a particular situation.[1]

Here some degree of tension was normal and to be expected. In another situation it is possible that lack of tension would be abnormal. Miss Young goes on to describe another interview:

An unmarried mother applying for admission to a maternity shelter was relaxed, smiling, unconcernedly cheerful. In the interview she said that

[1] Leontine Young, "Diagnosis as a Creative Process," *Social Casework,* XXXVII (1956), 279, col. 1.

she had been deserted by the baby's father, by her husband who was not the father, and by her family who wanted nothing further to do with her. Furthermore she had contracted a venereal disease. Under such circumstances her cheerfulness and lack of concern provided a warning signal that something was seriously wrong with the girl. This impression was later substantiated by other evidence which led to a diagnosis of psychosis.[2]

Always keeping in mind what the circumstances of the interview might be expected to mean to the client, there are some points of special importance to a diagnosis. Quoting again from Miss Young:

Focus on the person. The caseworker must begin by observing the person as a person—not as a case, a problem, or a category, tentative or otherwise. What does this person look like? Does he dress as if he cared for his body—or as if it were a despised or ignored encumbrance? Does he hold himself easily erect—or with shoulders slumped in defeat? Does he move with the comfortable ease of spontaneity—or with the stiffness of muscles rigidly constricted or the rag doll looseness of lassitude? Does he use his hands in spontaneous and illustrative gestures—or in endlessly repetitive mannerisms, in tension-propelled movements, or compelled quiet?[3]

How does the client express his attitude toward his problems? Not necessarily by the words he uses. The literal-minded worker who makes the mistake of assuming that the client knows what he wants and means what he says is likely very soon to find himself floundering in contradictions. But we can watch for clues which to the alert and experienced interviewer will provide an indication of the client's unexpressed feelings:

Opening sentences

The very first words a client says when he comes into the interviewing room may be indicative of how serious he regards his problem and his opinion of his own abilities to handle it himself: "I guess this isn't very important but I thought I'd ask you . . ."; or, "I could probably dope this out myself, but since I was in the

[2] *Ibid.*, p. 279, col. 2.
[3] *Ibid.*, p. 276, col. 1.

neighborhood . . ." Frequently, the interviewer gets an immediate indication of the client's attitude toward him or toward asking for help: "I may be in the wrong place, but . . ."; or, "I don't suppose anybody can help me but . . ."; or, possibly, "I wouldn't have come but So-and-So insisted . . ."

Association of ideas

The phenomenon of free association is well known to the lay public. . . . It is worth while to be aware of its operation both in the client and in the interviewer. When the client mentions something such as lying, divorce, a grandmother, there may be started in the interviewer a stream of association which has little to do with the client's feelings about these things. The interviewer must recognize his own associations, as otherwise they may operate unconsciously. That is, he may read into the client's problems feelings that he has but the client does not have.[4]

On the other hand, alertness to the client's stream of free association can provide a good many clues. A woman may be discussing her marital problems, and instead of continuing logically talking about her relationship with her husband, she may begin abruptly relating an episode remembered from her childhood concerning a quarrel between her parents. The caseworker is justified in assuming that the woman's feelings about her husband are tangled with her feelings about her parents. She may be identifying herself with her mother, or she may be thinking of her husband in terms of her father. In either case, this is the cue for the caseworker to open the way for the client to talk about her childhood feelings toward her parents, for in the light of those early attitudes her present feelings toward her husband may be clarified.

Shifts in conversation

It is frequently difficult to understand why a client suddenly changes the topic of conversation. The reason often becomes apparent through study of what he was previously saying and the topic he began to discuss. The shift may be an indication that he was telling too much and desires not to reveal himself further. It may be that he was beginning

[4] Garrett, *Interviewing, Its Principles and Methods*, p. 50.

to talk about material that was too painful for him to pursue, perhaps too personal or too damning. On the other hand, it may be that what seems to the outsider as a shift in conversation is really a continuation, that in the unconsciousness of the client both discussions have an intimate relationship. For instance, the interviewee may be discussing his difficulties with his foreman and suddenly begin discussing his childhood and the beatings his father gave him. The relationship in his own mind between the foreman and his father becomes obvious. Or he may be discussing his mother and suddenly make a personal remark about the woman interviewing him, indicating that in his own mind she in some way reminds him of his mother.[5]

Recurring references

A client may return persistently to a certain subject—how unfair his boss is, the difficulties with his wife, his own physical ailments. Sometimes the recurring references indicate only that the client's thoughts are stuck like an old-fashioned phonograph needle in a groove he cannot get out of. Then the interviewer must help him by introducing a new subject herself. Sometimes the choice of the new subject can be determined by something that has gone before —something previously mentioned but not explained, for example. Or the worker may have to insert something blindly, and watch to see whether the reference recurs again. Or he may be able to start the client thinking along more profitable lines by saying, "What would you like to do about it?"

Inconsistencies and gaps

Contradictions in the client's story may indicate guilt or confusion. Unexpected gaps in an otherwise straight story are often of particular importance. A man may avoid telling why he left his last job, or in relating his employment history may leave several months unaccounted for. A woman may discuss in great detail certain difficulties with her children but never mention her husband. The significance of such gaps becomes clearer through cumulative force. One such occurrence suggests a possible interpretation, and if ten others confirm it we have not a possibility but a probability.

[5] *Ibid.*, p. 51.

Concealed meanings

It is essential that the caseworker accustom himself to listening for the meanings behind the words. When an unattractive adolescent announces that she hates boys and loathes parties, the chances are that what she means is that she is very much afraid that the boys do not like her and that she will not have any opportunity to go to parties. Annette Garrett says:

Usually, however, the presence of concealed meanings is not obvious, and often it is only with the most careful observation of slips of the tongue and attitudes and other clues that the interviewer can obtain any increased idea of the client's total meaning. An unmarried mother who protests that she doesn't even want to see the father of her baby again may be concealing her infatuation for him and her hurt that he has "left her in the lurch." [6]

When an interviewer has reason to suspect a concealed meaning he should give the interviewee every possible opportunity for an open discussion. The concealment may be due to deliberate misrepresentation, or to an avoidance because of guilt, or to the client's own self-deception. If the interviewer can guess the real meaning, he may himself express it in a matter-of-fact manner as though that were what the client was saying all the time: "Of course it's hard not to be sure whether you're going to get a chance to go to the prom." "I know it's difficult when the man with whom you have been intimate isn't interested any more." Frequently, this approach is successful in persuading the client to accept the expression of a true underlying need, and in so doing, clear the way for more effective help. However, if the client does not accept at once the direct interpretation, probably the matter should not be labored. The client is not ready yet, and tearing away defenses will leave him exposed and helpless. Or perhaps he will deny it today and come back tomorrow accepting it and prepared to move on. But in either event, the caseworker should watch for the concealed meanings, and operate in relation to them, whether or not they are ever verbalized by the client.

[6] *Ibid.*, p. 53.

Perhaps a word of warning should be inserted here. Sometimes a young worker, especially one just beginning to be aware of the intricacies of psychiatric implications, will be tempted to over-emphasize the hunt for hidden meanings. Any number of stories illustrate this. Two young psychiatrists-in-training met a senior colleague as they entered the building. "Good morning," said the colleague. The two younger men proceeded in silence until one muttered, "Now I wonder what he meant by that?" Or, again, the story goes that in one of the large schools of social work the students have convinced themselves that you can't win. If you arrive ahead of time for an appointment, you are anxious; if you arrive on time you are compulsive; if you are late, you are resisting the appointment. But a caseworker must keep his head and his common sense. Not all stomach-aches are psychosomatic. Not every word spoken need be loaded with deep implications. And in some helping situations the hidden meaning, if any, might better be ignored. If a man is hungry he must first be given food. Donald Howard tells of an inexperienced and overeager caseworker in a public agency:

A man applying for assistance was asked by the worker about his feelings toward his wife, his wife's feelings toward him, his feelings toward his children and the children's feelings toward him, the wife's feelings about the children and their feelings toward her, and finally about his feelings about the children's feelings toward his wife. Thereupon the applicant said, "Lady, I only came here to ask for assistance." To this the worker replied, "But before we can help you we must understand you." [7]

Caseworkers must be sensitive and aware, but they must also keep their feet firmly on the ground.

Concluding sentence

The way a client closes his remarks is noteworthy. He may sum up what the interview has meant to him, or suggest the degree to which his own forces have been mobilized for action, or he may indicate continued hopelessness or undiminished antagonism. What-

[7] Donald Howard, "Public Assistance Returns to Page One," *Social Work Journal*, XXIX (1948), 115. Quoted by Leyendecker, *op. cit.*, p. 288.

ever he says at the end of the interview gives the interviewer an inkling of what to expect at the opening of the next.

Throughout any interview, the interviewer must listen sensitively to the words the client selects for self-expression. Leontine Young says:

> The caseworker must learn to listen to a person's language—his choice of words, his use of pronouns, the tense of his verbs. Does the client habitually make himself the subject or the object of his sentences? The person who says "I did" by his very words assumes responsibility for the action. The person who says "It happened to me" assumes no responsibility; he is by his own definition the victim of the action. The alert caseworker has already learned something valuable about the two persons speaking. The first, by his assumption of responsibility, has revealed some degree of healthy ego. With regard to the second, the caseworker's pertinent question concerns the meaning of "it." If the speaker means, for example, "The lightning struck me," the sentence makes sense. On the other hand, when an unmarried mother says, "I don't see how this could have happened to me" rape is the only possible circumstance in which the statement makes sense.
>
> In practice, the "it happened" construction rarely refers to anything as definite as lightning. Unfortunately it usually refers to nothing except the person's evasion of personal responsibility. Neither a caseworker nor anyone else can do much for the person who must always be the passive victim of "It happened to me" and never the subject of "I did." When a person who has usually been "me" is able to become "I," he has taken a step of great psychological import and his language faithfully records that fact.
>
> Children are aware of this and particularly of the useful service "it" can be when they are in a tight spot. Ask a child how the dish was broken and he is likely to tell you "It dropped." On his face is the bland and hopeful assumption that you will disassociate him from that comfortingly impersonal "it." The expression is one not unknown among adults who have been heard to say, "It didn't get done". . . . Almost everyone uses its services upon occasion, but when a person makes too frequent use of "it," or uses it in serious and important situations, that person is telling us that he has a real problem in assuming personal responsibility and probably is showing real ego damage.[8]

[8] Young, *op. cit.*, p. 276.

For the helping person, the diagnosis of the client's situation and of his personality potential must be a growing thing, subject always to review, correction, and expansion as new material comes to light through observation of behavior or through further interviews. The diagnosis should never be regarded as final and finished, with a Q.E.D. at the end. Every time the worker and his client meet, the diagnostic process must be renewed. That person who announces smugly that his first impressions are always right, and that he never has to change his first estimate of an individual, is deceiving himself and is not the person to give true help to another.

CHAPTER VI

Diagnosis before treatment

IN THE PRECEDING chapters we have described some of the techniques for discovering what manner of person the client is and what the problem may be. The need to learn the nature and extent of the problem is obvious. Surely no worker would dream of making a plan for his client until he knew whether the client's problem was loss of employment, a quarrel with his wife, delinquent behavior of his children, a need for hospitalization he cannot afford, or any one of the hundred other circumstances that may plague humanity. So much will not be argued. But perhaps the need to learn what manner of person the client is, needs more explanation and emphasis.

Florence Hollis says:

The treatment of any problem is inevitably determined in large part by one's understanding of its nature, and that, essentially, is what diagnosis is. In casework, diagnosis is the attempt to define as accurately and fully as is necessary for casework treatment the nature of the problem, its causative factors, and the person's attitude toward the problem.[1]

Perhaps the problem is a child's running away from home. That is a symptom, and any doctor knows that symptoms may look alike although they come from different ailments calling for different treatment. A child may run away for any one of a number of reasons, and here as elsewhere, motivation largely determines casework treatment. Perhaps the runaway finds that he cannot face an

[1] Florence Hollis, "Personality Diagnosis in Casework," a paper presented at a meeting sponsored by the New England Chapter of Smith College School for Social Work Alumnae Association, Boston, January 14, 1955; reprinted in *Ego Psychology and Dynamic Casework* (New York: Family Service Association of America, 1958), p. 83.

unbearable social situation. He is disliked by his schoolmates and he is unable to live with the awareness of such rejection. Or he may be, in reality, incapable of meeting the teacher's expectations in class-work, and unable to face a knowledge of failure. Or he may be escaping from expected punishment for a misdeed, or he may be avoiding the humiliating consequences of some embarrassing episode—he wet his pants in public; or, if he is considerably older, perhaps he carried the ball to the wrong goal posts and lost the game for his team. Or his running away may be a reaction to some real or imagined slight suffered at home, and he is prompted by the hope that "they'll be sorry when I'm gone."

No two runaways would be handled in the same way. Whether a slow child needs placement in an easier school grade, or whether some youngster from the wrong side of the tracks needs help in his social adjustment, or another needs clarification of the facts of family life or strength to face his childish humiliation, depends wholly on why the child did what he did. Only if the caseworker can diagnose the troubled one's personality, the circumstances, and the way he feels about those circumstances, can the worker know what help to give.

Take another example. Bill was in the fifth grade when it was learned that he was pilfering small sums of money and probably had been doing so for some time. Faced with the evidence, he showed no concern. His attitude implied that other kids had money, he wanted money, why shouldn't he take it where he could find it? A visit to Bill's home elicited the information that the mother was an alcoholic and had been arrested twice for shoplifting. The father was out of work much of the time, dependent on public assistance, and had served jail sentences for petty larceny. Here is a situation in which a boy is following a pattern established for him from his earliest years. The model of behavior which Bill has seen at home, and accepted, leads him to take what he wants in the easiest way. Punishment now might persuade him that it is wrong to steal, but on the other hand it might prove to him only that it is wrong to get caught. It would be much better, if possible, to provide him with a different model, to build in him a conscience more socially acceptable. A popular athletic coach, a scout leader, a teacher

whom he trusts, might do it. Or perhaps this goal will be too difficult to accomplish while the boy remains in daily contact with his
own family, and placement in a foster home or an institution is the
only answer.

But look at another boy. Norman was in the fourth grade when
he was found to be stealing. He had taken money, various small
articles, and, on one recent occasion, a bicycle. Investigation showed
his home to be in a moneyed neighborhood, the parents of excellent
standing in the community. The father had an exceptionally well-
paid position that kept him away from home much of the time. The
mother was an active clubwoman interested in numerous charities.
The intimate care of the boy had been left to servants. Both parents
were horrified to learn that their boy was stealing, and completely
bewildered. Why should he steal a bicycle? He *had* a bicycle, an
expensive English model given as a bribe to do better work in
school. "He's always had everything," the father said; "everything
a boy could want—toys, an allowance, summer camp, everything."
They had spent a fortune on Norman, they said, but this was the
end. They were humiliated. They would arrange to have him sent
away to a private school where he could be controlled. It would cost
another fortune, but they felt it was the only thing to do. So Norman was sent away to an expensive private school, and in less than
a year he was back, expelled for stealing.

Unlike Bill, Norman had been exposed to good standards at home.
He was not stealing because that was a way of life he had learned
from his parents, and he was not stealing things he thought he
needed—he had just as good ones at home. What he lacked was
neither a conscience nor things, but love and personal attention
from his parents. Confusedly, he was reaching for what all his life
had been the accessible symbols of love. Exile from home only
confirmed his sad suspicion that he was unwanted, that his parents
did not really care for him. Banishment did not correct his behavior.
Only a satisfaction of his unrecognized hunger for love and acceptance could have done that.

Motivation, however, is not the only factor to be considered in
forming a diagnosis and making a plan of help. Let us suppose,
for example, that three high school teachers have failed to receive

a renewal of contract. The criticism made of each was that class discipline was poor. Each of the teachers has a degree in education, and each is eager to find another position. But the interests and the skills of the three differ widely, and those differences would determine the plan suggested for each. One is a scholar, research-minded, interested in his subject matter but not in his students. His teaching was dry, too technical for his audience, failing to stir any enthusiasm, and his students, bored and restless, misbehaved in his classes. Another is a young girl just out of college. She is small of stature, timid in manner, with no self-assurance. Early in the year she had let it be seen that she was frightened of the big boys, and helpless when they rudely took over class activity. The third is a middle-aged woman, an experienced teacher who has for years been successful and well thought of, but who has recently been slipping badly. If the future is to hold success for these three people, three different plans must be made. Perhaps the man should not try to teach at all but should look for a research job. The young girl might be more successful with smaller children where her gentleness would be an asset rather than a handicap. Quite possibly the older woman should have a thorough physical examination to determine whether there is a medical reason for her decreasing efficiency. Perhaps she should think of retiring, or of turning to a job that demands less nervous energy.

Another factor that influences diagnosis is the racial and ethnic background of the client. As a caseworker studies his client he travels a narrow channel between the Scylla of ignoring very real racial differences and the Charybdis of explaining every quirk of behavior as due to race. A Negro client who shows antagonism for his white caseworker may be motivated by exactly the same impulses which could prompt a white client to resist a white worker —resentment of his own dependency, or identification of the worker with a hated father figure of authority, or any of the several other emotions which sometimes block easy relationship between client and worker. But the Negro client may also be showing an anger born of all the deprivations forced on his race by the white race. The caseworker must not take either explanation for granted, but must explore and watch for clues that will provide a hint on how to proceed. If the eldest son of a Japanese family shows a resistance to parental demands it may mean no more than it would if an American adolescent were making the customary clumsy efforts to establish himself as an independent person. But because of the traditional pattern of Japanese family life, it may mean a great deal more. Any caseworker must know something of the national and racial customs of the client with whom he is working, and consider to what extent these customs are affecting behavior and attitudes.

The social and educational background of the client also will help to determine the type of help which can be used, and therefore needs to be understood before a plan is formulated. In fact, cultural values must be held firmly in mind as the caseworker builds up his diagnosis. One woman who speaks of her husband as "a stinking bastard" may be using what is to her everyday language, and may mean nothing stronger than another woman means when she says her husband drank too many cocktails last night and embarrassed her at the reception. Moreover, the social background determines to a large extent the way in which the client himself regards his problem. One man accepts a loss of employment as the sort of thing that happens all the time to most of the men he knows. Work is seasonal, he will get another job presently, and meanwhile his vanity is not in the least threatened. All he needs is a grant of assistance until something else comes along. Another man with different training and different expectations of himself may be quite overwhelmed by a catastrophe which seems to him proof of his personal worthlessness. He needs another job but he also needs a great deal of emotional support to help him regain confidence. To take a third example, one girl may be crushed by the social disgrace attaching to her out-of-wedlock pregnancy. Another, from a different background, accepts her condition as quite the usual thing. Perhaps her own mother is unmarried, or many of her friends have borne out-of-wedlock babies. There is no stigma in her circle to such an occurrence. The first girl will need emotional support, possibly help in preserving anonymity, probably assistance in exploring the advisability of placing the baby for adoption. The second girl may need little more than help in securing medical advice, and later, perhaps, a grant from Aid to Dependent Children so that she can bring up her child.

Any medical man will agree that not only do not all diseases respond to the same remedy, but not all patients with the same disease will react in similar fashion to similar remedies.

Perhaps not the least important of the values derived from a thorough and honest attempt to diagnose causative factors behind a client's problem is the effect such a diagnostic study may have on the caseworker himself. A worker who comprehends the hampering mental and emotional disabilities against which the client is struggling will be less tempted to feel critical and judgmental. A situation which might be easy for the case worker to handle may present unsurmountable emotional obstacles to the client, and only if the caseworker understands these obstacles, and accepts them as authentic, will he be willing and able to plan a program of help which the client can use. Nothing is gained by scolding a vacillating woman for being unable to bring herself to sign a petition against her husband for support. A shortsighted caseworker might see only the financial advantage of forcing a wayward husband to provide for his family, but the wife may be quite unable to face a life without a man at her side to direct her every move. Maybe loss of financial support is as nothing to the loss of emotional support. Only if the caseworker recognizes the woman's dependency will he see how futile it is to criticize and blame.

An awareness of the client's inner personality will have another effect on the caseworker in that such awareness can save him from reacting as though what the client says or does is directed at him personally. He will not be offended if a client fails to show appreciation of the efforts made in his behalf, or if he does not respond to the worker's well-intentioned attempts to establish a friendly relationship. Rather, the worker will recognize the possibility that the client may be unable to relate to anyone, that he is not rejecting the worker personally but may be afraid of any attachment to anyone, having once been hurt by someone he trusted. A caseworker in his professional life must be as objective as a physician, accepting unpleasant or antisocial behavior as symptomatic of a disorder in no way directed at him.

A clear and accurate diagnosis helps the caseworker maintain perspective and objectivity. It guides the selection of the plan of help. It will also help the worker determine at what point to seek advice from another discipline. A faculty adviser once told a college freshman that she should give up all thoughts of graduating, and look for a routine factory job. He based his diagnosis on her lethargic manner and overweight and on the fact that her grades since Christmas had been mediocre and were growing worse. He meant well; for any student should be directed away from an enterprise for which he has inadequate physical or intellectual endowment. But in this case the diagnosis was incomplete. What the adviser failed to take into consideration was that the student's high school grades had been excellent, and in September when she entered college she had been an active, alert person. The adviser's recommendation might have crushed the girl's hopes, and in fact did give her an unhappy three weeks during which she was convinced that she was no good whatever. Then a routine medical examination revealed that she had developed a hypothyroid condition. Medication corrected this, and before June she was back to normal and able to sail through her examinations with high honors. If that faculty adviser had taken the trouble to look more carefully at the girl's record, if he had been sufficiently experienced to recognize what her lethargy might indicate, he would have sought medical counsel at once and saved the girl weeks of depression and discouragement. A slow reaction, delayed response, apparent retardation, may have a physical basis that can be corrected by medication, or these reactions may be due to an emotional block rather than to any mental inadequacy. Very often medical and psychological examinations and perhaps psychiatric tests are needed to determine the cause of apparent dullness and retardation.

There are some conditions, too, which it would be actually dangerous for a caseworker to attempt to handle without expert advice —the impulses of a psychotic, for example. A psychosis is a symptom of a patient's break with reality. The psychotic impulses cannot be reached or influenced through any normal approach; for the psychotic's frame of reference is false, often fantastic, and not to be guessed by someone whose logic is directed by reality. Inept efforts to work with psychotics may very well bring on an exaggeration of the symptoms and push suicidal or homocidal patients completely over the edge. The illogical and unreasonable suspicions of a paranoid patient, for example, are nothing to argue with. A paranoiac, following his own distorted logic, may decide without warning that someone is a mortal enemy even though that person has always been a close and well-loved friend. A violent attack on the victim may follow, with lightning speed and tragic results. Or a psychotically depressed person may abruptly become suicidal and do himself a fatal injury.

While a caseworker will not be expected to treat a psychotic, and indeed should never attempt to do so, there are some situations in which it is important that he be able to recognize the meaning of psychotic symptoms. Since facilities are at a premium in the overcrowded hospitals for the mentally ill, patients who are unlikely to harm themselves or others are often returned to the community on convalescent leave where they remain as long as they can function. But such patients may still be out of contact with the world around them, their behavior and their reactions difficult for the uninformed layman to accept. Then an understanding caseworker is needed to help the confused patient adjust and to interpret his condition to family and neighbors.

It is important for a caseworker to be able to recognize psychotic symptoms and be able to decide quickly at what point those symptoms indicate a need for help from an expert. This is true in working with patients on convalescent leave who sometimes experience a relapse. It is also true in working with the healthy person when behavior and attitudes may point to the threat of a possible psychosis.

We can do no better here than quote S. Mouchly Small, M.D.:

The following are some behavior changes to watch for in identifying a potential personality disorder:

1. A marked change in habitual personality reactions is one of the most important warnings of the onset of a psychiatric disorder. It is not so much the type of reaction as how much it varies from the individual's usual personality patterns that is important. If he was previously shy, seclusive, and reticent, and now becomes overfriendly, overactive, and

overtalkative, greeting everyone on the street, it may signify an impending excitement. Such obvious changes are important in persons who have previously been seclusive, but are of less significance in individuals who have always been sociable and friendly. It is the change in attitude that is the determining factor.

2. Peculiar behavior or mannerisms, such as constant shifting of the head from one side to the other, continuous mumbling or muttering, or sudden onset of a certain type of motor activity not usual for that person may be indicative of an impending emotional disturbance.

3. We may find a marked decrease in a person's efficiency without any apparent explanation. This may be due to preoccupations with underlying emotional conflicts, difficulties in concentration, impairment of memory, lack of persistence, or poor organization of work. Any of these factors may be early symptoms of a personality disorder. At times one may see a temporary increase in efficiency as part of an incipient elation.

4. The appearance of undue argumentativeness and irritability is often a sign of impending disorder. Argumentativeness to a certain degree is expected, especially when discussing emotionally charged subjects like politics or religion.

5. The development of almost automatic hostility to any suggestion is serious, particularly when the hostility begins to express itself in the form of jealousy or suspicion. That may be the first indication of a developing paranoid trend in which the person begins to suspect other individuals of making derogatory remarks or persecuting him.

6. Hypersensitivity to criticism where it previously did not exist may also be an indication of a personality problem. This may be associated with the loss of self-assurance and self-confidence.

7. A marked change in one's ambition without any change in the situation to account for it may be symptomatic of an emotional disorder. If this change is based on good reasons or if the goal is redirected because of practical considerations, it is not of serious prognostic import.

To evaluate these danger signals properly a knowledge of the individual as he formerly functioned in the community is absolutely essential. It is only through a comparison of his present behavior with previous personality functioning that relative changes may be adequately assayed.[2]

Once there is reason to suspect the presence of a psychotic condition, the caseworker's job becomes one of interpretation to the

[2] S. Mouchly Small, *Symptoms of Personality Disorder* (New York: Family Welfare Association of America, 1944), p. 9.

family. He must persuade them to accept medical advice and possibly hospitalization for the patient, try to make them see that this is an illness which needs treatment just as tuberculosis or a cardiac condition would need treatment, help them work through the feelings of guilt and shame which so often overpower the relatives of the mentally ill and prevent them from doing the sensible thing, which alone can help the patient.

CHAPTER VII

Adult maturity and immaturity

AS THE CHILD becomes the man, his emotional life proceeds through stages that merge imperceptibly just as do the phases of physical growth and those of mental development. First he is a helpless infant wholly dependent on his mother, and then he is a toddler ignoring authority and stumbling into all kinds of trouble as he investigates life. In an incredibly short time he is off to school, and the day after that he is an adolescent, driving the family car and dating the girl next door. And then, all at once, he is grown up and eligible for the draft.

Ordinarily, the physical, the mental, and the emotional aspects proceed toward maturity more or less simultaneously, but it is always possible that one of the three may suffer a temporary slow-down, or even a permanent blocking, while the other two forge ahead. Physical underdevelopment can be spotted at a glance, mental slowness is measured without much delay, but emotional retardation is far more tricky to identify and, unhappily, far less likely to arouse sympathetic understanding. One is tempted to be impatient with a gawky boy of fifteen who is as tall as his father but has no more sense of responsibility than a fifth-grader. However, one should not be cross with him. A sense of responsibility comes with emotional maturity, and lack of emotional maturity is a factor equal in importance with physical or mental underdevelopment, and quite as much beyond the reach of argument or exhortation.

Anyone who wants to help another must be able to determine with certainty whether he is working with an adult or with an immature individual who looks like an adult but may at any moment start behaving like an infant. It is, unfortunately, very easy to see maturity where it does not exist. Emotionally childish people may unintentionally fool us for months, so that we are led to expect too much of them and feel frustrated and critical when they fail us. A college sophomore may be the star of the debating team but still have ten years to live through before he will begin to be secure within himself. A wife and mother may have an easy, sophisticated patter, but still be as unstable as an adolescent. Nevertheless, in spite of the difficulties, if one is to work successfully with people, it is imperative that one be able to evaluate the degree of emotional maturity of the individual. Otherwise, one would never know what behavior and emotional reactions to expect and could never know what plan of help would be useful.

There are some qualities which we may confidently seek in a truly mature person. A mature person has emerged from the dependent phase of infancy when he has moved from the taking into the giving stage, and finds pleasure in giving as well as in receiving affection and emotional support. We expect a mature person to mingle with others in a friendly and sociable manner, as a member of a community. He is able to take another person's interests to heart, be friendly, sincere, sympathetic, aware of the effect his behavior may have on the mood of the group.

We also expect a mature person to live with an eye to future values, not for the present alone or for immediate pleasure. The adult has learned to refuse that last drink for the sake of a clear head tomorrow, to stick with a tiresome job this year for the sake of promotion next year.

We expect a normal adult to have ambitions and a goal in life, and that goal should be realistic in view of the individual's abilities. A mature person should know himself sufficiently to make the most of his capacities, neither avoiding effort through lack of confidence nor embarking on enterprises at which he must fail through lack of qualifications. (In psychiatric language, this means that he has a "realistic ego image.")

A mature person can deal with facts as they are. Either he accepts the situations in which he finds himself, adjusting to changing circumstances with a reasonable degree of flexibility, or, if he does not accept his circumstances, he works planfully to change them. He is not crushed by occasional failure, nor completely shattered by the blows of fate. He knows that he can either cure, or endure.

In short, a mature person is resilient, realistic, and able to accept responsibility. However, as every caseworker knows, many persons who live to a ripe old age retain to the end the emotional reactions of childhood. It is these people whom he must learn to recognize and with whom he must often work.

A failure of normal maturation comes about because one or more of several unfortunate things may have occurred along the way to retard development. Brain damage may inhibit mental growth. Both illness and lack of proper nourishment may slow up physical growth. Similarly, a damaging emotional experience or lack of emotional nourishment may cause an individual's emotional development to stop short of maturity. It is the job of any worker to recognize emotional immaturity in a client and plan accordingly. There is no more purpose served by trying to argue an immature person into assuming responsibility than there would be in scolding a mentally retarded child for not making top grades in school, or an invalid for his inability to do heavy manual labor.

One type of immaturity which a caseworker often encounters is that found in the neurotic individual. A neurotic often (though not invariably) recognizes his symptoms as unreasonable, but whether he does or not he still cannot correct them. The neurotic is what he is because of an inner lack of security, an inability to put faith in his own personality and his own worth. The insecurity, however, is expressed in an indirect fashion not always recognizable as insecurity by either caseworker or client. The neurotic person feels vaguely and disturbingly guilty without any rational explanation for the feeling. Or he is terrified of heights, or of cats, of closed places, or of open space, sometimes to the point of physical involvement such as sweating, breathlessness, or nausea. A neurotic may eat compulsively when he is not hungry, or he worries himself sick when his reason tells him there is nothing to worry about, or he feels a dread of something which he has no cause to dread—a serious illness he does not have, an unlikely catastrophe. Neurotic symptoms are impossible to control by conscious effort. It therefore does no good whatever for the caseworker, or friend, or member of the family to try to reason with the patient who quite possibly intellectually comprehends his condition but still cannot do a thing about it. The neurotic is uncomfortable, often exceedingly so. He can sometimes be helped by psychiatry but never by argument or logic. Meanwhile, he needs understanding of his discomfort and uncritical acceptance of his compulsive behavior. In fact, acceptance without fuss or comment may at times operate to reduce the severity of the symptom.

Most of us at one time or another have exhibited mildly neurotic symptoms. We are afraid of harmless garter snakes, or we get up in the middle of the night to be *sure* we turned off the gas. But until a neurosis reaches crippling dimensions it might better be left alone, by client and caseworker alike. Probably the caseworker's role should be one of interpretation and support to the worried or exasperated family of the client.

Another, and to the caseworker a more troublesome, type of immaturity is that known as the "psychopathic" personality, not by any means to be confused with the psychotic. The psychopathic, sometimes called the individual with a "personality disorder," takes little account of consequences and almost no account at all of the effect his behavior may have on the comfort or behavior of others. The psychopathic person may walk out on his obligations. He is likely to quit his job the instant it becomes boring or difficult. He leaves his family and does not worry about the future of his wife and children. He shows a naïve expectation that things will work out to his advantage without any effort on his part, and he is outraged and astonished when they do not. He haunts welfare agencies seeking public relief, and for the sake of his family it is usually provided. He commits traffic offenses because he has little concern for the rights of others. He is often AWOL from the armed services. He is frequently involved with the law for minor misdemeanors. He grasps immediate pleasures and cannot take the long view. He will not submit to even momentary frustration. He may be a drug addict or an alcoholic because of his impulse to escape from any unpleasant reality. He has the self-centered, conscienceless attitude of a child. Any worker in a family-serving agency is all too well acquainted with the psychopathic personalities who undoubtedly take up a disproportionate amount of his time and energy. The "hard-core families" who appear again and again on the case loads of every agency in the community are often fathered by the psychopaths with behavior disorders.

Here as elsewhere, before a plan of help is decided upon, the diagnosis must be right or irretrievable damage may be done. Symptoms of the psychopath can sometimes be confused with those of certain types of psychoses. In some instances the chief difference discernible to the layman is that the psychotic behavior is a sharp departure from the person's habitual manner, while a psychopath has behaved in the same way since childhood. Also, it must be kept in mind that seemingly psychopathic behavior may actually stem from a physical condition that could be corrected by medication. When in doubt, call in an expert, medical or psychiatric.

However, once mental illness and physical condition can be eliminated as possible reasons for an individual's behavior and the caseworker is convinced that he has a psychopath as a client, then he can only do his best in a difficult situation for the client's family. He must be careful not to succumb to the temptation to punish the family for the unadmirable actions of the psychopath. Children need food and care even if the irresponsible alcoholic father who should support them is exasperatingly failing to do so. The worker must be courteous and patient with the client himself, not, of course, condoning his standard of behavior, but not wasting energy with futile argument or useless admonishment, not losing patience or permitting himself to sink into discouragement when weeks and months and years show no improvement in the psychopathic personality.

Sometimes, for the safety of the community, a psychopath must be temporarily locked away from society. However, his stealing, his traffic offenses, his drunken brawls, are usually not serious enough to warrant lengthy imprisonment at public expense, and it is not to be expected that punishment will ever change his behavior. Such an individual is reacting to a self-centered impulse born of an unsatisfied emotional need. It is probably a need of long standing, dating perhaps from childhood deprivations, but by the time he is chronologically adult the response has usually become so habitual, the attitude so deeply internalized, that even if a tardy satisfying of the emotional need were possible, it could not appreciably change the behavior.

However, acceptance of the client as an individual—acceptance, that is, not of his behavior but of his needs—and a sincere effort to understand his needs will sometimes bring the client past whatever it is that has been blocking his growth to emotional maturity and help him become the adult he should be. True, this does not happen often, and no caseworker need be disappointed if he tries and fails to bring his client to maturity. But it does happen just often enough to make it well worth the effort to discover what the unsatisfied need may be and to try as far as possible to fill that need.

CHAPTER VIII

Common human needs

THERE ARE FOUR basic needs common to all humanity: the need for affection; the need for security; the need for achievement; the need for acceptance in a group. From the day of his birth to the day of his death, every mortal is striving in one way or another to find satisfaction for one or all of these needs. Obviously, the methods employed will vary widely with differences in age, emotional maturity, social and educational backgrounds, skills. A four-year-old may feel a tremendous surge of achievement when he first ties his own shoelaces; an eighteen-year-old, when he makes the varsity team. Achievement comes to an adult in one social or educational setting with the completion of a bit of tricky research; in another, with the successful outcome of an important business deal. A farmer knows achievement when a good crop is safely gathered; a woman, perhaps, when she has prepared an appetizing dinner for the man of the house.

What an individual expects of himself and what type of effort he puts forth to satisfy his basic needs are influenced in part by the current opinions of those around him, but even more are his patterns of behavior determined by the attitudes he absorbed during his formative years. In Chapter VI we met Bill, who was learning from his parents that stealing was an acceptable way of life. If the pattern were not changed for him, his sense of achievement in later years might well depend on "getting away with" some especially outrageous bit of thievery. By the time a boy has become an adult, his attitudes have become so internalized, so much a part of himself, as to be almost wholly unconscious—and this pertains to much more than his attitude about legal right and wrong. Sometimes, unhappily, these unconscious attitudes are more of a hindrance than a help in the struggle to find satisfaction. For example, an adult is usually able to satisfy his affectional needs through marriage, but if as a child he was taught by a finicky mother that sex is dirty he will probably always be uneasy in the marital relationship. In turn, this lack of emotional ease, persisting in the face of all subsequent intellectualizing on the subject, may well prevent him from finding fulfillment through marriage. Or, again, if a man was aware throughout his childhood that he was unwanted, that his parents resented his existence, he will find it difficult to appreciate his own value in any group situation. As a result he may withdraw, or he may bluster; either way, he will find it hard to win any satisfactory sense of belongingness.

More often than not, a person fails to recognize the nature of his own emotional need. The man who is unable to accept a sexual relationship may blame the tensions in his marriage to his wife's poor housekeeping or to financial worries. A teen-age boy who has failed to win acceptance in his group is quite likely to be defiant about it, announcing loudly that he couldn't care less—who wants to be a part of that dumb gang anyway! A man who has been fired from three consecutive jobs may be quite unable to face the fact of his own inadequacy and so stoutly affirms favoritism on the part of each new boss. All of us, caseworker and client alike, at times try to protect our cringing selves from the unwelcome knowledge of our own inadequacies and the grim awareness of a need that can never be met. Then we use the comforting mechanisms of defense. We repress a longing which we have been taught is shameful, we project on someone else the blame for our failures, we rationalize our less desirable behavior, persuading ourselves that we told our neighbor an unwelcome truth "for her own good" and never because we have a mean streak in us that finds satisfaction in another's discomfiture.

Some types of defense mechanism are healthier and more desirable than others, but it is improbable that the choice of mechanism is ever determined by social desirability, or even by common sense. Rather, the choice grows out of circumstances, the inner strengths or weaknesses of the individual, the models he has watched during childhood, and the expectations of his community. One boy who suspects himself of physical cowardice and inadequacy may compensate by a great deal of bragging and bullying because that is the kind of behavior accepted and admired by his group. Another boy in another environment might compensate by making an extra effort to excel scholastically. Sometimes a caseworker can redirect a client's energy into more profitable defenses, but this is not done merely by talking about it. A scrappy child who can be induced to discharge his pugnacity through organized sport is more happy within himself because of the regard in which he is held by others and the sense of accomplishment he feels in helping to win a game and the sense of belonging to a team, but this shift from fist fights to football will not be brought about merely by the caseworker's talking to him of his subconscious aggressive urges. The worker must know what he is doing, and why, but he must not discuss it with the client.

The universal habit of concealing our yearnings from ourselves and denying our undesirable impulses means that the real nature of the emotional need is something that a caseworker must uncover with little or no help from the client and often in spite of him. But until the emotional as well as the practical need is met, with the caseworker's help or without it, there is small probability that the client will be able to mobilize his capacities or establish any adjustment between himself and his circumstances. However, if the caseworker is able to see past the façade, he can often manipulate the environment so that the emotional need can be met in a socially desirable way. The scrappy child who is introduced to sports is one example. Another is the case of Mr. Kelso.

Mr. Kelso had been a successful landscape gardener with a business of his own until he became crippled with arthritis. When his savings were exhausted he applied for Aid to the Disabled, and for home relief for his wife. Mrs. Kelso, a woman in her fifties, was untrained for outside employment and, in any case, needed in the home to care for her husband. The grants were issued, but in visiting the home the caseworker came to realize that the man's unceasing and often unreasonable demands on his wife were reducing her to a state of nervous exhaustion. Twice in one year Mrs. Kelso became so ill that she had to be hospitalized. Mr. Kelso obstinately refused to permit himself to be moved to a nursing home during her absences, but hobbled about the house managing very well by himself. However, the instant his wife returned, he resumed his insistence on unremitting service. His wife must bathe him, dress him, fetch and carry for him, tell him the time of day, report on the weather, prepare snacks at all hours of the day or night. When the caseworker protested that Mr. Kelso was wearing his wife out and that he had already proved that he could take care of himself if he had to, he gave verbal agreement, but a moment later resumed his demands.

Because it was becoming increasingly apparent that Mrs. Kelso could not continue doing all the work in that house and wait on Mr. Kelso too, the caseworker suggested that they move to a smaller place. Mrs. Kelso agreed with a sigh of relief. Mr. Kelso, who was enjoying himself, protested, but in the end a compromise was reached, and the Kelsos moved to a small first-floor apartment in a two-family house owned by a widow who occupied the upper apartment alone. There was a large yard, and the caseworker, remembering that Mr. Kelso had been a landscape gardener, mentioned to the landlady that she could consult him about planting and caring for the yard. He not only gave good advice, but offered to do some of the work himself. Two weeks later the man who had claimed that he must depend on his wife for every personal service, who had done nothing for himself when he could get someone to do it for him, and who had shown no impulse whatever to do anything for anyone else, was hobbling slowly but usefully about the yard trimming shrubs, outlining new flower gardens, keeping busy all day, while landlady and neighbors exclaimed over the amount of expert work this crippled man could accomplish. The more they exclaimed, the more effort he put forth and the more he managed to do. The wife was freed from the unceasing demands; the man found satisfaction in the recognition given his efforts and his skills; the landlady had a handsome, flower-filled yard; the welfare agency was relieved of the expense of recurring hospitalizations for the previously overburdened wife; and everybody was much happier.

This is a success story, a success that came about almost by accident. If the caseworker had been more alert to the nature of Mr.

Kelso's emotional needs, she might have arranged sooner the environmental manipulation that satisfied the needs. When Mr. Kelso's failing health obliged him to give up his own landscape gardening business, he lost the recognition which his achievements had given him. His demands on his wife were his efforts to force from her a recognition of his accomplishment in the field of invalidism, complicated, probably, by a desire to return to the infantile pleasures of dependence on a "mother." His efforts were selfish, silly, and completely unsuccessful, but the need was very real and very human. When the need was satisfied in a fashion more acceptable to everyone, the casework aim of helping a man adjust to his circumstances was met.

A young, inexperienced, and somewhat prosaic caseworker in a public welfare agency was having difficulty with Mrs. Horton, a client who was never satisfied with the amount of her grant. The grant had been figured in accordance with the budgetary standards of the agency so that the woman was receiving for herself, her disabled husband, and her child an amount comparable to that issued any family in similar circumstances. But Mrs. Horton insisted that the caseworker was discriminating against her. The worker repeatedly and somewhat impatiently explained agency limitations. He made out menus and shopping lists, informing the client that if she followed these in her meal planning she would be all right. But nothing helped. Mrs. Horton complained at least once a week. The caseworker felt that she was a psychopathic individual impossible to satisfy.

Then the case was transferred to a more experienced caseworker, who listened sympathetically to Mrs. Horton's tale of woe about food costs, her husband's insatiable appetite, her child's increasing demands, her own "nervous" stomach. This casewoker did not mention budgets or the amount of the grant. Instead, he said, "I know how you must feel. It's difficult, isn't it, to have all the responsibility of taking care of everyone else when there isn't anybody to take care of you?" Mrs. Horton's antagonism dissolved in tears. Yes, she sobbed, that was just it. She'd always had it hard. She'd been obliged to take care of somebody ever since she was a child. Her mother had been an invalid, her father a demanding bully. She'd thought it would be better when she married, but then her husband became disabled, and her child was too young to be any help, and she had it all on her shoulders again. She nearly went crazy with both of them leaning on her all the while. The caseworker said he could see how it would be. Perhaps Mrs. Horton would like to come to the office and talk things over once in a while. It might help just to talk.

That, of course, was exactly what Mrs. Horton had been trying to do, but the first caseworker's failure to understand had kept her on the defensive. Mrs. Horton did not need more food nor did she need more money to buy food. Although perhaps she did not know it herself, and certainly could not express it, what she needed was someone to understand the trouble she was having struggling to be mature enough to take care of a crippled husband and a small child when she herself was a dependent sort of person with emotional needs still unmet. When a caseworker recognized that need and met it in part, Mrs. Horton stopped the repetitious, time-consuming complaints about the food budget, and used her appointments for more practical discussions of how to get along on what she had.

The initial activity of any worker confronted by a new client must always be to discover the external facts and cope with any practical problems the situation may present. No amount of sympathetic understanding of Mrs. Horton's emotional needs would have been of the slightest help if she and her family had actually been hungry or dispossessed from their home. But once the practical demands are satisfied, the caseworker must go deeper if the client is to be helped toward a lasting adjustment to his circumstances.

However, no caseworker, in any social agency, operates entirely alone. Every community has some helpful resources. We have recently begun to realize how closely all the helping professions are bound together. Poor schoolwork may be a result of poor health. So may marital difficulties and financial problems. On the other hand, all physicians recognize that some health problems originate in emotional tensions. So it goes. All types of help are interrelated, and a worker must be aware of the possibilities of calling in another profession to supplement the aid that he can give. Suppose, for example, that a man goes to a welfare agency for financial assistance because he has lost his job. The agency will grant him aid if that is his urgent need, but any long-term plan of help should inquire into the circumstances behind the immediate situation. Perhaps he lost his job because it was the wrong one for him, demanding qualifications he did not have, or failing to use skills he did have so that he was bored or ashamed. That calls for consultation with the company's personnel director or with an employment agency. Or the man may have an outspoken resistance to authority because of old, half-forgotten difficulties with an overstrict father. Again, a different sort of job, one in which he is somewhat removed from direct authority, may solve the problem in the future. Or perhaps he failed because of poor health and needs medical care. Or the failure may stem from marital difficulties that use up so much energy that he is unable to operate efficiently. Then perhaps he would benefit from a marriage counseling service. Or he may be weighed down by an unexpressed guilt over an old sin that should be brought into the open with his priest or pastor, who could give him the spiritual help which alone can relieve him. Or he may be depressed to the point close to suicide that indicates a desperate need of psychiatric help.

In these and similar circumstances a worker will, first of all, use the technique of environmental manipulation to meet the practical, external need. He will use his knowledge of human personality to discover and meet as far as he can the emotional needs. He will almost certainly, if he is an effective caseworker, apply the technique of supportive relationship. But he will not, if he is wise, ever attempt to be all things to all men. He will turn to other agencies and other disciplines to secure help for the client, help that will supplement what he or his agency can offer.

And so we turn now to ways in which referrals to other agencies can best be accomplished.

CHAPTER IX

How to make an effective referral

A PERSON who has found himself in trouble, financial, emotional, or legal, is likely to turn to a friend or professional acquaintance, or to an agency about which he has heard. If this is his first experience, the troubled one may by chance turn to an agency that cannot meet his particular problem, but the caseworker to whom he tells his story must hear him out. Anyone who has accepted a profession that claims to be a helping profession has accepted the obligation to listen to a person who comes to him in trouble. It may be evident fairly early in the interview that the troubled one has come to the wrong place for the special help he needs, and if that is the situation, then the worker must direct him to an agency where help is available. The caseworker will listen to him, ask questions, and through this initial interview diagnose as far as possible what the problem is, the way the person feels about the problem, and what if anything he has already done about it, and what he hopes still can be done.

This initial interview and the resulting diagnosis are known in most agencies as the "intake process." In a large organization the whole job of one or more persons consists of seeing new applicants when they first come in for help. In smaller agencies the intake is usually done by staff members who have other responsibilities as well. Either way, it is important that anyone who undertakes an intake interview should be skillful in creating an atmosphere in which the client can open up and talk freely. The intake worker should also have a thorough knowledge not only of the resources and limitations of his own agency but also of other resources in the community. If the agency can help with this particular problem, the intake worker will start at once formulating some sort of plan with him, but if the client mistook the functions of the agency, then the intake worker must refer him to the place where he can find help.

The intake worker may close the case in his agency at the point of intake, transferring the whole problem, lock, stock, and barrel, to another agency. This might happen, for example, if a boy should go to a school nurse for help in finding a summer job. The nurse would probably send the boy and his request to the school guidance director, or to an employment agency, along with any information about the boy and his abilities that she might have. Or, if a man worried about his sick child should go to his pastor, the minister might call in a doctor, or send the man to a clinic, or possibly, if there was also a problem of money to meet the medical bills, to a public welfare agency.

At times, however, the one who sees the client at intake may hold open the case, giving through his own agency what his agency is equipped to give, and applying to resources in the community for additional help in areas beyond the scope of his organization. This would happen, for instance, if a man applied to a public welfare agency for help in placing a mentally retarded child in an appropriate state school. An agency worker would refer the child to a psychologist for accurate diagnosis, and if placement were recommended by this source, he would make a further referral to the institution selected and help the family through the legal procedures for admission.

It is impossible that any one agency should be equipped to meet unaided all the varieties of problems that may be presented to its intake worker during the course of a year, or even, perhaps, during a day. Let us look, for example, at the situations met in the intake office of a large family-serving agency.

A mother comes in with a spastic child. Authorities have told her that he needs some sort of education, but clearly he cannot get along in the rough-and-tumble of public school, she cannot possibly pay for a tutor, so what can she do, she asks. Or perhaps the child is blind, or deaf, or epileptic, or mentally retarded, or hampered by any of the handicaps that make public school life intolerable and pointless for a youngster. The mother needs help in planning for him.

A shiftless-looking man lounges in. He has lost his job, the unemployment insurance has not started yet, he has no savings, rent is due, and there is no food in the house. He needs help right away, he says, or his furniture will be put on the street.

A hesitant seventeen-year-old girl comes to the agency. She is pregnant, and terrified that her father will find out. Her mother knows, but she too is afraid of the father. The girl has six months to wait before the baby will be born, and where can she go? She does not know what to do about the baby, either. The man was a cross-country truck driver, she does not know where he is now, and she does not want anything to do with him any more even if she finds him.

The judge of the Children's Court phones to refer a fifteen-year-old boy who has been taking joy rides with other kids in stolen cars. The judge feels that this boy was never a leader in the gang, that he is far from incorrigible, but that his family is quite incapable of coping with him. The boy would probably straighten out with a little help. Is there any place for him to go, not quite so rugged as a state correctional school?

A seventy-year-old man fumbles his way into the office. He assures the worker that he is just as smart as he ever was, but it seems that nobody wants to give him a job any more, so how can he earn an honest living? He has always done odd jobs, so he does not have any Social Security, but he cannot get odd jobs now because he cannot work fast enough to suit people. His daughter-in-law will not have him in her home. She claims he scatters tobacco in the bed, and he likes to sit in the living room where the television is but her daughters want to entertain their dates there and do not want him around. Nobody wants him around. So where can he go?

An exhausted-looking man collapses in the client's chair. He has hitchhiked from a city 300 miles away because he heard there was work here, but he has looked all day and cannot find anything. He needs a place to flop for the night, and he needs help to get back to his family.

A school nurse telephones. A high school girl badly needs dental work. Her teeth are in shocking condition, a menace to her health and an embarrassment to her because of their appearance. Both her social life and her schoolwork are suffering. Her family are not on relief, but they cannot afford the extensive work required. Can the agency do anything for her?

A distracted mother comes in carrying a small baby and dragging three other preschoolers behind her. Her husband has walked out. The electricity is turned off because the bill has not been paid, and there is not much food in the house. She would work if she could, but how can she leave the kids alone? And she could never make enough to pay a baby sitter. Cannot somebody make her husband do what he ought to, and cannot somebody help her with the bills meantime? She does not want to "put the kids away" if she does not have to.

The hospital telephones. A migratory worker has been brought in by ambulance with a bad knife wound in his side. Who will pay the medical bills?

A farmer calls up. Does the agency know any husky boy who could help with chores in return for his keep? There would be no wages, but the boy could go to school, and there would be plenty of food.

A harried man comes in. His wife is going to have another baby pretty soon, and he does not see how he can take care of the two kids already at home. There is no relative who can help, and although he has looked around for a woman to stay with the children there does not seem to be anybody. If he stayed home with them himself he would lose time from his job and he might even be fired. The boss does not like men who do not appear regularly. Is there anything the agency can do, just for a week or so, until his wife gets back on her feet? The children are four and two, good youngsters, but too little to be left alone.

With some of these situations a family agency can help directly. With others, it cannot. Clearly, the intake worker must have at her finger tips information about educational resources for the handicapped, and medical resources for those who are afflicted by all sorts of physical and mental disabilities. He must know the employment possibilities in his community, and how to help the unemployed by referral to employment agencies or with information concerning applications for unemployment assistance or retirement benefits or survivors' benefits, or for home relief if none of the other resources is applicable. He must know about service clubs, neighborhood clubs, Travelers' Aid, court resources. He must know about foster homes, visiting housekeeping services, visiting nurses. He must know all the social agencies, public and private, both their potentialities and their limitations.

The list of resources that follows can do no more than suggest, since resources vary from state to state, from county to county, from city to city. However, from this list the person who hopes to help a client can select whatever is both suitable and available.

HEALTH PROBLEMS
    Clinics
        Cancer
        Cardiac
        General medical
        Pediatrics
        Tuberculosis
    Loan closets for invalid equipment such as crutches, wheel chairs, and hospital beds
    Nurses
        Insurance company
        Private
        Public health
        Visiting
    Private medical or dental practitioners
    Public health officers
    Special committees
        Cancer
        Heart
        Muscular dystrophy
        Tuberculosis
    Special hospitals
        Cancer
        Epileptic
        Mental
        Tuberculosis
HANDICAPPED
    Associations for the blind, state and private
    Itinerant teachers

Private schools for special handicaps
    Cardiac
    Mentally retarded
    Spastic
Rehabilitation programs and training centers
State aid for the handicapped child
State schools for special handicaps
    Blind
    Deaf
    Mentally retarded

FINANCIAL NEED
    Fraternal organizations
    Private relief organizations
        Church-related
        Secular
    Public welfare agencies
        Child welfare
        Public assistance for adults or family groups
    Special need
        American Legion
        American Red Cross
        Legal Aid
        Travelers' Aid
        Visiting homemakers

LAW ENFORCEMENT
    Courts
        Children's
        County
        Domestic relations
        Supreme
        Surrogate
    Police department
    Probation and parole officers

CHARACTER-BUILDING GROUPS
    Boy Scouts and Girl Scouts
    Campfire Girls
    Church groups
    Community houses
    Future Farmers and Four H
    Home and Farm Bureau

Neighborhood clubs
Y.M. and Y.W. Christian Associations and Hebrew Associations
MENTAL HEALTH
    Clinics
        Child guidance
        Mental health
    Psychiatrists
    Psychologists
    Public or private schools offering therapy
EMOTIONAL PROBLEMS
    Agencies offering casework and marriage counseling
    Psychiatrists
    Religious leaders

It is of the utmost importance that the person who makes the referral should know exactly what he is talking about. In addition to a pretty clear picture of the client's situation, the worker should have a thorough acquaintance with the resources, and the regulations of the agency to which he is referring his client. Imagine the frustration of some unhappy individual who is shunted from agency to agency, only to be informed by each one that he is not eligible for the type of help provided there. Repeated rejection is certain to aggravate any problem in the mind of the sufferer.

Many institutions, both state and private, can accept applicants from only a limited geographical area. There are often age limits, or requirements concerning the intelligence quotient of an acceptable client. Private organizations sometimes accept clients of only a specified religious faith. Most of the state schools and private institutions offer brochures which outline their services and their regulations. Many of them give explicit directions which should be followed in making a written referral before sending a client on to them.

A referral may be made to an agency or an institution at some distance, but more often it will be to a resource in the community. It is wise for anyone working with troubled people to acquaint himself not only with the resource agencies but also with the personalities of the staff members of those agencies. No organization is more helpful than the people who run it want it to be, and the special slant of any agency is determined by the director and the staff. In one community a pastor or a priest may keep himself available to anyone in trouble, while in another the leaders of those same denominations may limit their activities to their own people. In one area a public agency may do adoption work; in another, it does not. Some school vocational guidance directors serve also as counselors in personality problems; in other schools they limit their work to advice on employment. Some Salvation Army Corps operate shelters for transients; some maintain workrooms where second-hand furniture is refinished and sold for very little; some specialize in collecting inexpensive clothing; some, in serving hot soup to the indigent. It all depends on the special interests or skills of the personnel, the funds of the Corps, the greatest need of the vicinity. As the worker gains experience and puts down roots in his own community he will learn which individuals and which organizations can be called on for the particular type of help needed in any situation. The wider and more personal his knowledge of area resources and organizations, the greater his value to his own agency and to his clients.

When a worker refers a client to another individual or another agency, whether for complete care or for help to supplement that which is already being given, he should first get in touch with the person to whom the client is referred. Sometimes this can appropriately be done by phone; more often it should be done in writing; possibly it may be done by a telephone call that is followed by the detailed written referral. This is one of the many times when a caseworker benefits from the kind of imagination which enables him to put himself in the other fellow's place. What sort of information does the intake worker of the second agency need in order to make this interview as easy as possible for the client? What should the referring worker say that will lead the other worker to ask just the right questions that will put the client at ease and prompt him to tell his whole story?

There are three questions, the answers to which the intake worker of the second agency should always be given:

1. What is the problem as the first worker understands it?
2. What is expected or hoped for from the second agency?
3. How does the client feel about the referral? In other words: how has it been interpreted to him by the first worker?

If the case has been closed by the first agency at point of intake and the client referred at once to a second agency, these questions may be the only ones which the written referral can cover. But if the client has been known for some time to one agency and is referred to another organization for supplementary service, a great deal more information will be available and as much of this should be given to the second worker as could be considered helpful toward quick interpretation of client or of problem.

By way of illustration, suppose we outline the information which might profitably go with a child referred by a school to a child guidance clinic from whom psychological testing, psychiatric diagnosis, and recommendation are expected:

1. Description of the present problem
2. Present school life
   a. Scholastic record
   b. Scores of mental or aptitude tests
3. Physical condition
   a. Defects of hearing, seeing, breathing, coordination
   b. Known permanent effects of old illnesses, operations, or accidents
   c. Tendencies toward colds, sore throat, indigestion, nervousness, constipation
   d. Marked physical weaknesses
4. Social record in school
   a. Participation in school activities
   b. Friends: Number? Age? Type?
   c. Adjustment to fellow students:—Is child a leader or a follower?
5. Life outside school
   a. Meals: Regular? Adequate? Quality?
   b. Sleep: Regular? Adequate?
   c. Exercise: Type? Effect (stimulating; enervating)?
6. Home
   a. Housing
   b. Cultural facilities and standards
   c. Religion
   d. Number of children
   e. Outsiders in the home: Relatives? Boarders? Servants?
   f. Attitude of child toward other members of the household
7. Family background
   a. Father
      1) Age

      2) Health
      3) Personality
      4) Occupation
      5) Education
      6) Religion
      7) Interests outside the home
   b. Mother (same information as for father)
   c. Siblings (same information as for parents, where applicable)
   d. Attitude of members of the family toward child
8. Early history of child
   a. Physical history
      1) Duration of mother's pregnancy
      2) Health of mother during pregnancy
      3) Birth history: instrument used; any difficulties; weight
      4) Method of feeding: breast or bottle; feeding difficulties
   b. Early childhood
      1) At what age did he walk? Talk? Teethe?
      2) Toilet training: At what age? How accomplished?
      3) General health
      4) Childhood diseases
      5) Shots and immunizations
   c. Emotional history
      1) Fears and anxieties
      2) Tantrums
      3) Shyness
      4) Delinquencies
9. Attitude of parents toward present problem
10. Attitude of child toward present problem

This may seem to be an unnecessarily detailed outline, but every item in it would help the psychologist and the psychiatrist to a deeper, truer understanding of the child, thereby enabling them to make a recommendation based on an accurate diagnosis. All of the facts needed to complete such an outline could be obtained through interviews with the child's family, his teachers, school nurse, school doctor, family physician and guidance director.

In other situations, less information would be required in order to make an efficient referral. A person sent by an agency to apply for a job, for example, might be accompanied or preceded by an outline that gives:

Name
Sex
Age
Education
Medical record
Previous work history
References from previous employers
Anything that has transpired since the last employment which might
    affect present employability
Special skills
Special handicaps
Attitude of the employee toward this referral

Each referral must necessarily be different, each outline adjusted
to the individual circumstances of the special referral. But the two
included here are sufficient to show that what every worker needs in
making a referral to another agency or another worker is: (1) knowledge of his client and the client's need; (2) knowledge of the other
agency's rules, requirements, and limitations; and (3) an imagina-
tive awareness of what the worker in the other agency needs to
know so that he may help the client promptly and efficiently.

Nor should the client himself be forgotten in the process of referral. He must never be left with the impression that he is being
shunted from spot to spot without being consulted and without explanation. Any referral from one caseworker to another carries with
it some slight implication of rejection, and this must be minimized as
much as possible. The rejection may be very slight indeed. A man
perhaps goes to a social agency quite well aware that this organization is not equipped to help him but hopeful that he can obtain information about other resources: "I know you're not the ones that
find people, but my boy left home last week. He's nineteen and
probably all right, but I just wish I could hear about where he is."
"My old father is getting very queer in the head, and I just don't
know how to go about getting him put where he can't do himself
an injury. Can you tell me what I have to do?" In such cases straight
factual information is all that is needed. But often an applicant
comes in hoping for help, expecting it, unaware that he has come
to the wrong agency for his purpose. Then it may disturb him very
much indeed to be sent elsewhere, the depth of the hurt depending

on the seriousness of his trouble and on his own temperament. An insecure person might give up and not seek help again even if another address were given him.

Perhaps the client is to be sent to another agency, or he may be transferred from one division to another within the same agency, or perhaps he must be transferred from one caseworker to another because the first one is leaving the agency or taking a holiday. Then the referral must be carefully and tactfully made, with complete explanation to the client of the reasons, whether due to agency organization or more personal matters concerned with an individual worker. Even when reasons are given and all explanations supplied, the client may still have a nagging suspicion that the first agency, the first division, the first caseworker, really wanted to get rid of him. There are three practical suggestions for helping a client overcome this feeling: Explain the transfer in terms he can understand. Give him a chance to say how he feels about the referral, which will help him express any resentment or hurt he may feel. And see to it that he has a definite appointment with the second agency or the second worker, an appointment explicit as to day, hour, and place. In fact, the first worker should accompany him and make the introduction, if that is at all practicable.

CHAPTER X

Casework in public assistance

THE TERM "CASEWORK" has been used with different meanings in two different contexts, a fact which quite naturally tends to produce confusion in everyone's mind, including the caseworker's. In one context, the term is used to describe a specific service, namely, psychological counseling directed toward diagnosis and treatment of personality difficulties that interfere with an individual's ability to maintain constructive and satisfying social relationships. This type of casework is used by the highly trained staff of psychiatrically oriented private agencies to help disturbed individuals clarify their problems and interpret their own inner confusions and inadequacies.

In another context, the term "casework" is used to describe a general method of administering a number of social services, such as the grants under various categories of public assistance. As a casework method it must include an acceptance of the client as an individual with his own unique attitudes, impulses, and feelings, but it does not seriously attempt to change those attitudes.

The second meaning is the one implied by the civil service title of "caseworker" given to members of the staffs of public assistance agencies in many states, and it is with the second meaning that the word is used in this book.

The most unfortunate result of the confusion of terms is that people who have a hazy idea of what psychiatric casework can sometimes accomplish, and no notion whatever of the peculiar problems involved, expect far more of a public assistance caseworker than he can possibly produce. The confusion may even be true at times of the caseworker himself who, not understanding the training and disciplined skill required for psychiatric counseling, is repeatedly baffled and frustrated by the dismal failures of his own conscientious and misdirected attempts to change human behavior.

Casework in a public agency cannot work toward changing behavior except indirectly and as a happy by-product of other more direct services. Hilary Leyendecker summarizes the welfare job as follows:

1. To provide financial assistance in appropriate amounts to all needy persons whose eligibility for that assistance has been verified and to withold assistance where need is not sufficiently acute by agency standards.

2. Through understanding of the individual causes of economic dependency, and the limitations and capacities of the needy person, to help him insofar as that is possible to return to a condition of self-maintenance.

3. To determine eligibility and to administer assistance and related services so that the experience can be a constructive one for the needy person—one wherein his capacity for self-direction is maintained or strengthened, one in which he can face the disagreeable reality of his dependency without accepting it as desirable or inevitable or feeling personally degraded by his misfortune.[1]

Perhaps the chief technique (though not the only one) applicable to casework in public assistance is environmental manipulation, a technique that demands knowledge of community resources and a skill in discovering which of these resources the client needs and can use. This implies that the caseworker needs more skill in counseling than might at first be supposed necessary.

Often applicants who are in real and verified need resist agency regulations. Many agencies demand that an applicant for Old Age Assistance should give the agency a lien on any real estate he owns. In return, the agency issues the grant of assistance, pays the taxes on the property, keeps it in repair, and permits the client to live there as long as he is physically able to do so. After the client's death the property is sold to reimburse the agency in part for the assistance given. Although this would appear to be a way of eating one's cake and having it too, still it is sometimes hard for the needy person to accept or understand the arrangement. One client was heard to say tearfully that she had "gone in her calico rags" to keep her home

[1] Leyendecker, *Problems and Policy in Public Assistance*, p. 240.

free from mortgage and she would not give up now—and this despite the grim fact that she was weak from malnutrition, that her home was big and drafty and exceedingly inconvenient. To that woman a lien or a mortgage was a symbol of defeat, and weeks of tactful, friendly interpretation were necessary before she could accept the inevitable without a feeling of degradation. Again, most public agencies insist that legally responsible relatives should be interviewed and that any available resources over and above those needed for their own immediate family should be applied to the requirements of the applicant. But old people do not like to be dependent on their children, especially if the children are not very hospitable to the idea of supporting an aged parent. It has happened that an old mother has gone hungry and cold rather than permit her son to be interviewed.

An agency caseworker must operate within the framework of his agency. He must understand and accept its regulations, and he must be able to interpret them to his clients. He cannot authorize assistance where eligibility requirements are not met, but he has failed in his duty if he has not explained and interpreted the requirements to the client, and if he has not done his very best to present them in a way that enables the client to accept them as reasonable and necessary.

Often a caseworker meets behavior and attitudes that call for a great deal of understanding of human motivations before any decision can be made concerning eligibility for assistance.

Mrs. White was left a widow with four small children. The insurance money, handled with discretion, would have maintained her and the children for nearly a year. Instead of budgeting the money, however, she squandered it in a month, buying things she had longed for all her married life—new linoleum for the kitchen floor, a modern refrigerator, a washing machine, a dish washer, a shiny bedroom suite, a television set, new clothes all around. She also went on a movie spree, purchased expensive toys, and bought food extravagantly. When the money was gone, she applied for Aid to Dependent Children, for which, as a widow with minor children and no income, she was technically eligible. True, she had no resources, but can public funds rightfully be used to support a woman who could have supported herself and her family for a long time if she had managed differently? Or, should she be punished now for what is over and done with? Worse yet, should the children be made to suffer for what the mother has done?

Mrs. Black is another widow who was left with two children and insufficient resources. In response to the caseworker's questions she reluctantly admitted that her parents owned their own comfortable home and would probably have room for her and the children. If she moved in with them her small payments from Social Security's survivors' benefits would be sufficient, and she would not need an additional grant from the agency. But her relationship with her father had always been poor. She remembered him as a harsh man and she knew that he disapproved of her marriage. He would certainly not now refrain from loud and bitter criticism of Mr. Black. She did not want her children subjected to this. They loved their father, and would be even more upset by the grandfather's attitude than they already were by their father's death. Besides, they would probably get on their grandmother's nerves. A finicky woman, absorbed in her housekeeping, she would not be tolerant of the noise and confusion, the finger marks, and the tracked floors inevitable when there are two healthy children in the house. The atmosphere in the home would be tense and edgy. Must Mrs. Black go there, to the possible detriment of her children's adjustment to their fatherless life? Or should the agency authorize a grant of assistance in spite of the fact that there is a resource in her parents' ability to take her in? Almost certainly, the taxpayer who foots the bill for assistance, unaware of the tensions in the home of Mrs. Black's parents, will be highly verbal in his opinion of what should be done.

Or think of the situation we met in our Introduction—Sam Brown, who cannot hold on to any job, maybe because of inborn laziness, maybe because of a "lifetime of poor nutrition, or rotting teeth, of bad eyesight, of a profound but unrecognized discouragement." Or Sarah Smith, the mother of four out-of-wedlock children by different fathers, two born since she began to receive public assistance payments. Or Bill Jones, who has deserted his wife and three children, is living with another woman by whom he has had three children, and cannot support both families. Should Sarah Smith's children suffer for the mother's behavior? Should Mrs. Jones be denied assistance because it is her husband's responsibility to support her?

With dismaying frequency the caseworker finds himself facing a need to plan for such a person or for the family of such a person. Clients with personality disorders make up the smallest proportion of any worker's case load, but undoubtedly they manage to create the largest amount of adverse publicity, calling down on the caseworker's luckless head public criticism no matter what decision he makes or what he does for or about them. A caseworker cannot expect to change the behavior of such as these, but he needs some understanding of human motivations and personality development in order to accept these situations without exhausting himself with doubts of his own adequacy when a client persists in self-destructive behavior.

There are those beset by age and misfortune. An old man finds he has outlived his years of active usefulness. He always supported himself, but he was never very clever and he never made much more than it took to keep himself fed and decent day by day. He is willing to work now, but he has arthritis, and his eyes are not so good as they were, and he cannot seem to keep up with the amount of work the boss thinks ought to be done. Now he is beginning to feel that he is of no use to anyone, that nobody wants him, that he no longer has anything to contribute. The manner in which the caseworker carries on the investigation of eligibility, the way in which he interprets the agency regulations, the thoroughness with which he explains the basis on which the amount of the grant is determined—all these can give the man a supportive relationship which is the essence of good casework. Quite possibly there will also be a need for manipulation of the environment as the old man is helped to find satisfactory living arrangements, secure adequate medical care, and perhaps start an interesting hobby.

A husband and father abandons his family and cannot be located. The wife is left with small children and no resources. Perhaps for the first time in her life she is called on to handle money, pay the bills, keep to a budget. For the first time she has no one to whom to turn for decisions, for planning, for strength. Worst of all, she must face the realization that her husband has chosen a way of life that does not include her. She needs financial help from Aid to Dependent Children, but even more she needs a supportive relationship with someone who understands and accepts her confusions, her muddled efforts to manage her affairs, her crushing feeling of personal failure, her guilt and resentment.

Here again the worker's manner, his acceptance and understanding, is a vital part of the casework, just as much as the issuance of the needed grant of assistance. Almost everyone who applies to a social agency needs a supportive relationship—not enervating sympathy, but acceptance as an individual with personality and problems separate from the personalities and problems of all other clients. The aged, the blind, the disabled, who must somehow face a life that is woefully different from the life they carelessly took for granted in their rugged youth; the mothers who are widowed, deserted, or perhaps were never married; the wage earners whose jobs have collapsed or whose work is seasonal—they all need help, emotional as well as financial. Sometimes their predicaments are the result of their own inadequate or distorted personalities, but that does not make any of it one bit easier to endure.

The caseworker who is aware of the common human needs, and who can keep clearly in the forefront of his mind the disastrous things that may happen to a personality when those needs are not met, is the caseworker who can do the best job.

CHAPTER XI

Casework in child welfare

IN MOST AREAS of this country there can be found either a protective agency, such as the Society for the Prevention of Cruelty to Children, or a division of the local public welfare organization, called by some such title as "Department of Child Welfare." Or there may be both. If the abuse or neglect of a child is reported, a worker from one or the other of these agencies will investigate. Sometimes the report is unfounded. A jealous relative or a neighbor annoyed by childish racket has made the complaint from spite. Or someone with good intentions has been precipitate. Three-year-old Jimmie, supposed to be taking his nap, has slipped out when his mother's back was turned and is happily making mud pies in the road, naked and content. Or an emergency has called both parents away from home, leaving four small children for an evening in the care of a ten-year-old sister—not advisable, but not a cause for breaking up a home if it is done once because of some unavoidable circumstance. The investigating worker, satisfied that there is no ground for action, will report back to the complainant and try to calm the neighbors.

Sometimes bad conditions are caused by inadequate income. Today most people know of the existence of unemployment insurance, survivors' benefits from Social Security, home relief, Aid to Dependent Children, but if ignorance or pride or some special circumstance has stopped a family from applying for the help to which they are entitled, the caseworker can try to interpret to them, and get the ball rolling. There is no reason today to remove children from their own homes for financial reasons only.

However, sometimes bad conditions are not brought about by lack of funds but by ignorance or insensitivity on the part of the parents.

Adult though they may be chronologically, perhaps they have not the maturity to assume family responsibilities without help. Or they may have emotional needs so deep that their attention must center on themselves, leaving nothing to give the child. Or they may be inconsistent in their discipline and unable to control an unruly youngster, or their own standards may be antisocial. Or they never wanted children anyway, and show their rejection in a number of damaging ways which stir the child to responsive undesirable behavior patterns.

Sometimes a caseworker can effect rehabilitation of such a home without removing the child, and if he can, he will do just this. The upright members of the lay public sometimes show an unfortunate impetuosity in recommending removal of children. Slovenly housekeeping, too few baths, poor eating habits, unemployment, poverty, drunkenness, immorality on the part of the parents, have all at one time or another been regarded as cause for taking children from their home. Today, assistance can meet financial need. Poor housekeeping, dirtiness, and bad diet often are corrected by better housing, advice from dietitians, help from a trained homemaker, and such aids should always be offered before there is any thought of breaking up a family.

Drunkenness and immorality demand more careful consideration. If the drunkenness results in physical abuse, if the immorality means that the child is brought up to accept antisocial behavior, then perhaps placing the child is the wisest thing to do. But only perhaps. Any agency worker knows that there are not enough foster homes, nor enough money in the welfare budget, to accommodate all the children of all the parents whom the upright would like to punish because they go on a roaring drunk every Saturday night, or live without benefit of clergy. Moreover, it cannot be forgotten that some drunks are affectionate parents in their sober moments, able to give a child the security of knowing he is loved and wanted. Some unmarried couples live together with more stability and mutual respect than some who have gone through the most elaborate church ceremony. If poor housekeepers cannot or will not learn, if fathers cannot stay sober, if parents can but will not get married, then the caseworker must pause and consider whether the child will be more damaged by dirt and the unbalanced diet, by seeing his father drunk, by knowing his parents are not married—or by losing the security of a home he is used to, where he knows he is wanted. On the other hand, if he is not wanted, if he is not loved, if he is rejected openly or subtly, then another home where he can find affection and security is the best gift that could be offered.

If the parents truly love their child in their fashion, then the caseworker must try to correct whatever is wrong with the home. If it cannot be corrected, then he must think twice—or three times, or five times—before he decides that removal of the child is the step to take. A foster home is better than no home, but there is a feeling in every child for his own parents, no matter what they are like, for which there is no adequate substitute.

A child in foster care is like any other child, with the same impulses and the same emotional needs, but foster children have almost always had a bad start in life or they would not be in foster care. Moreover, placement in a foster home presents a number of special hazards from the child's point of view. There is always the chance that if he does not conform to what is expected of him the foster mother will exclaim, "I don't have to stand for actions like that and I'm not going to. Back you go to the Welfare!" Or a foster mother may, unwittingly, let a child see that his board money does not pay for the food he eats, and he just better behave himself and help around the place if he expects to be kept. But if a child has to earn his position in the home by model behavior, can it be called a home? Robert Frost says:

"Home is a place where, when you have to go there,
They have to take you in." "I should have called it
Something you somehow haven't to deserve." [1]

Even if a woman takes a foster child into her home, not for money but because she loves children, still she is the exception if she does not convey by implication that he ought to show his gratitude by being the kind of child to whom she can point with pride. For the child there is an unnerving reality to this subtle threat of rejection. It has happened to him once. It can happen again. Such a child

[1] Robert Frost, "Death of the Hired Man," in *Selected Poems* (New York: Henry Holt and Company, 1923), p. 13.

knows very well that he can be sent back to the placement agency to be shipped out again into the unknown. The whispered comments of neighbors, the remarks of other kids on the street, the sometimes unfortunate attitude of school authorities, all combine to keep him aware that somehow his own parents failed him, perhaps did not want him, and just maybe it was his own fault and maybe the foster parents will not want him either. It takes a lot of concentrated reassuring to overcome the nagging awareness of all that, and it is the unusual foster mother who is able to give the extra love and assurance that are needed day in and day out. Some foster children never get it.

If, in addition to this hazard, the foster child has a vivid memory of early deprivations in the home of his own parents, if the removal from his own home was sufficiently recent that he remembers the time when all his foundations were knocked out from under him, when he did not know what was happening, or why, or what was going to become of him, then nothing in his life is solid or sure or wholly to be trusted.

Even if all this happened when he was such an infant that he does not consciously remember the events, the effect on his personality can be damaging. Psychologists are pretty well agreed that there is no such thing as too much security during infancy. A baby is wholly dependent. He cannot satisfy his hunger without assistance, but must always wait for mother. If her arrival is too long delayed, or if she comes to him feeling tense and edgy, he will be uncertain just what to expect from life. Doctors for some time have recognized that hospitalized babies need more than medication. If they have only that, they may respond physically, but they show psychological damage. Every baby needs someone whom he recognizes as his own special mother-person, who will love and cuddle him. Every baby needs the emotional reassurance that can come only from knowing there is in the world one person happy to take care of him, to come when he is hungry or uncomfortable, to help him when he needs help. The habit of doubt and insecurity that may develop if the infant does not have such reassurance may last on into adult life long after the man has quite forgotten his infancy. It will certainly color his feelings and reactions while he is a child so that if he goes into a foster home after badly deprived early years he cannot at once trust the foster parents no matter how warm and loving they may be. He may continue to act like a bully to shore up the sagging foundations of his independence long after there is any real need to do so. Or he may be stiff and withdrawn, utterly unable for a long time to respond to affection. Or he may, once his defense begins to break, try out his new parents in dozens of ways, all of them exasperating, fairly defying the foster parents to keep on loving him no matter how badly he behaves. This is the time when a good many foster mothers, astonished and hurt, give up and ask the agency to move the child—exactly the worst thing that could happen, confirming as it does his very darkest suspicions that he is not really wanted anywhere.

Children will not be able to put their doubts and longings into words. Perhaps they will not even be consciously aware of what they want and what they need; or, if they are aware, they may be impelled to dissemble exactly as grown-ups do. Sometimes a good amount of imagination must be exerted if one is to see beneath the surface. But a good caseworker responds to what is meant rather than to what is said. A young lady member of the casework staff of a social agency was walking home alone one evening when a very small boy, a stranger to her, slid his hand into hers. "If you're going my way," he said, "maybe I better walk along and protect you." There was only the tiniest tremble in his voice to indicate that what he really meant was, "I think maybe I'm a little scared and it would be nice to walk with a large grown-up, just in case." What the caseworker did then was responsive to what he meant. She closed her hand firmly over his and remarked that she had just that minute been thinking how much better she would feel if there were a nice boy to walk with her. So they proceeded through the dusk, the small boy's self-esteem undamaged by any need to reveal openly his timidity.

Sometimes a child, unable to find the intangible that would satisfy an emotional need, will turn to a concrete object as a symbol. Norman, who stole money and a bicycle he did not need, was doing that. And there was a little girl who persistently stole soap. Not pennies, not toys, not candy. Just soap. Finally, a sensitive adult realized that the perfume of the pine soap reminded the child of her mother, who had died the year before. She wanted the soap to hold in her hand when she went to bed in the dark. For her, as for Norman, the object stolen was a symbol. Eventually, that little girl found security in her foster home, but meanwhile she had needed the comforting reminder of a mother's love.

If a child has remained beyond infancy in a rejecting home or in one where the standard of behavior is not good, the youngster's habits may be anything but acceptable in his new environment. A number of influences may have gone into forming a child's pattern of behavior, not all of them necessarily the influences of a socially substandard home.

A very small child has no concept of right or wrong. However, as soon as he is sufficiently developed to be aware of forces outside himself, he will begin to see the advantage of behaving so as to win approval and avoid punishment. If the parental standard of behavior is consistently presented, the child will begin in time to incorporate that standard within himself so that he feels the urge to do what mother wants whether mother is there or not, and he feels uncomfortable doing what he conceives as wrong even if there is no probability of discovery and subsequent punishment. This internalizing of standards comes about partly through habit strongly established, and partly through the child's emotional identification with the parent figure, an identification which always operates if the parent-child relationship has been emotionally satisfying.

If the parent's standard of behavior is erratic and inconsistent, the child may grow up too confused to establish any workable ideal for himself. We then have a youngster who truly does not know right from wrong. He is in danger of having no firm standard of behavior, no conscience, no feeling of guilt in defying the established community pattern. Then we are very likely to have first a juvenile delinquent and later an adult criminal. Fortunately, it is possible that a child from a home of poor or inconsistent standards may identify with another adult, a relative, a teacher, any hero he may select as his ideal. In that event, his conscience will be an internalization of the standard acquired from this new relationship. Unhappily, this process can operate downward as well as upward. If well-meaning but too permissive parents are weak and inconsistent in teaching their child standards of behavior, that child may later attach himself to a "hero," and it will depend on chance and his environment whether he selects a socially acceptable figure or the town bully who can teach him delinquent behavior.

It sometimes happens that upright parents who love their child very much will, with the best intentions in the world, maintain a standard so impossibly high that he never can meet it. For the sake of winning parental approval the child many make the attempt, but if he never wins the approval, he may react strongly, even violently, against this impossible standard rather than face repeated failure and self-criticism, and we have then the "minister's son and deacon's daughter never doing what they oughter." It is a background such as this that produces the phenomenon which so puzzles and outrages the general public—a delinquent or near delinquent from "one of our very best families."

It is to be remembered that while some of an individual's personality traits—his aggressiveness, his willfulness, or his compliance, for example—are probably largely inherited, his conscience, his concept of what is right and what is wrong, is always the result of environment. It must also be remembered that though conscience operates to some extent in all human beings, the behavior it prompts will vary greatly in different cultures. The child of a middle-class American family may have been taught kindness to animals until it is almost a physical impossibility for him to lift his hand in abuse of a dumb creature. On another level of culture, a child may absorb the attitude that beating an animal is no different from picking a flower or felling a tree. One civilization puts high value on human life; another feels that failure to avenge any personal affront by killing the offender is an indication of cowardice. Each man's conscience is the outgrowth of the cultural climate in which he lives. We cannot expect the same standard from a Fiji Islander, a mountain hillbilly, an Eskimo, a Boston blue blood, a Mohammedan, an East Side tenement kid, a Harvard medical student, a Mid-Western farmer. They do not expect the same of themselves. Each has his conscience which, if healthy, will prompt the behavior appropriate to the culture in which it has developed. An educated Chinese lad will not feel the same toward his parents as does an educated American boy. The acquired conviction of what can be accepted and what cannot, affects attitudes toward an amazing range of human interests—diet, personal adornment, the number of baths that one should take each week, premarital sexual experience, family loyalties, civic responsibility, respect for other people's property, types of religious ceremony; the list is endless.

It takes tolerance and understanding on the part of both foster mother and caseworker to accept the sometimes rebellious behavior of a foster child who is making the adjustment required when he finds himself transported into a foreign element. He may think: "At home Pa used to give the kids a swipe across the side of the head, and it only meant that for once he was paying attention to us. In this place all anybody does is talk, talk, talk, and maybe nobody really cares. At home there was none of this sissy business of sitting at table, saying grace, using a napkin, saying 'please' and 'excuse me.' At home nobody sat down to any table. The kids just grabbed a hunk of bologna or a store cookie when they were hungry, and maybe here it doesn't matter to anybody if we get hungry between meals. At home *of course* everybody said whatever was necessary to say so as not to get licked. Here folks talk about telling the truth, but wouldn't that be just plain silly when it would mean a walloping, or, worse yet, getting sent off to bed before the television show is finished!"

All children in foster homes have problems that derive from their past experiences, the uncertainty of their future, the comparative insecurity of their present. Although every situation is a little different from every other, and each child is a separate personality, still there are some reactions that appear so often that they can almost be termed characteristic of foster children. The caseworker must help the foster mother meet each problem as it appears, he must interpret to her the child's unlovable behavior, giving the foster mother understanding and with it patience to endure or correct. It helps quite a bit to know what to expect.

One reaction, and probably the most difficult with which to deal, is bed-wetting. It does no harm to arrange a medical examination to rule out any possible physical cause, but almost always the cause of enuresis is emotional. It accomplishes nothing for the foster mother to scold, punish, shame, or reduce the child's liquid intake.

When the child feels safe, when he feels at home with the foster mother, bed-wetting will stop and not before. Months of patient reassurance from both foster mother and caseworker may pass before that time arrives.

Another common reaction is swearing and the use of dirty words. The child's background may be responsible, of course, but sometimes even if he knows better he will come out with his "damns," and worse, as a form of testing: "They say they want me. Do they mean it? Will they keep me even if I say things they don't like?"

Other annoying reactions are those of sneering at everything about the foster home and bragging about his own home. Louise Raymond is writing for adoptive parents who have taken older children into their homes, but she might well say the same to foster parents:

They'll tell the wildest tales about what they used to do, to the neighborhood children as well as to you. Sometimes these yarns are fantasied extensions of your own home—"Oh, a piano, sure—that's nothing. Where I came from they had a piano in every room, even the bathroom." Or he may embroider in the most clashing colors he can find. He drank, he says (and maybe he did!), he smoked, it was nothing for him to go to a night club with another fellow a couple times a week. All this is very hard on parents who, while they are hardly looking for expressions of appreciation, can't help expecting a pleased reaction to their pretty home and the new room they fixed up especially for him. But you won't really mind any more once you stop to think that this child is fiercely fighting off pity. He has to show you he's no dog begging for crumbs—he's just as good as you are. And this too will pass, so long as you don't ridicule his pretendings or call them lies or show him in any way that you think he's a pretty lucky kid and he'd darn better be grateful.[2]

Spells of whining, tantrums, frequent crying, are far from unusual when foster children first come to their new home. Nightmares, indigestion, picky eating, may also be expected, but all of these manifestations will gradually dwindle and finally disappear as the child becomes convinced that he is safe.

Another type of behavior which is hard for foster parents to understand is the so-called "negative transference" of which more will be said in another chapter. If a child has been misused, neglected, or rejected by his own parents he may well feel bitter and resentful

[2] Louise Raymond, *Adoption and After* (New York: Harper, 1955), p. 137.

toward them, but because he has such a heavy stake in the parent-child relationship, because he wants so desperately to be accepted by his mother and father, he does not dare show his resentment to them. Perhaps he does not even admit it to his conscious mind. But then, when he finds himself in a parent-child relationship with people who are not really his own family, all the bottled-up bitterness comes out. It will be safe now, he feels, to let it spill over since it is not directed toward his real parents. A kindly, loving foster mother will be puzzled and dismayed when her foster child for no reason that she can see kicks her in the shins and screams, "I hate you! You're a horrid mean old thing!" The kicking must be stopped, forcibly if necessary, for violent behavior directed at really hurting people must be controlled, but the verbal expressions might just as well come out. Eventually, if the foster mother can last, the child will drop the transference and begin to see the foster mother as herself instead of as a representation of a rejecting parent. Perhaps the chance will come for the caseworker to say casually to the child, "Maybe it isn't this mommy you hate. Maybe somebody else made you mad a long time ago." Sometimes this brings the youngster into reality, but if it does not, better let it go and let the child work things through at his own pace.

Meanwhile, still another hazard must be faced by most of the children in foster homes. If his own parents are dead, which is not often the case, the child can imagine parents to suit himself. Usually, their own parents are alive, and in most states they have a legal right to visit; in any case, the placement agency will work toward eventual return of the child. So after the child is in his foster home, the parents visit, often with unsettling results. The own parents, having failed, project their guilt on the foster mother, and naturally they resent the individual who is succeeding where they failed. This reaction is so universal as hardly to need mention, but it often astonishes and hurts the foster parents who have naïvely been expecting praise and gratitude. But gratitude is almost never found in situations such as these. The own parents are immature—if they were not they would have been more adequate parents in the first place—and since they are immature, their resentment is not controlled. They try to woo the affection of the child back to themselves with criticisms of the foster home, with extravagant and impossible promises of wonderful gifts to come next week, sometimes with attempts to win the child's sympathy for their own misfortunes and grief. Unless the foster mother has an unusual degree of insight, she may be tempted to retort to criticism with countercriticism, to comfort the child for broken promises by calling the own parent, more or less politely, a liar. At best, this sort of parental visit leaves the child torn, and if the foster mother does not handle the situation with restraint and tact, the whole affair can be damaging in the extreme.

A foster child needs acceptance in his community, like any other child. In the foster home he needs reassurance of security and continued acceptance—more than children who are in their own homes, because a foster child can take nothing for granted. He needs someone to help him work through the conflict of loyalties. He needs to talk about his fear and his resentment at what life is doing to him. Often his dread of rejection in the foster home prevents him from talking freely there, but every child needs someone who will not be shocked, will not scold, will not threaten, but will just listen while he talks out the tensions which can react so unfavorably on his behavior.

The caseworker must relate to the child, remaining his stanch friend no matter what, making it clear that he can always talk freely to him and that no harm will come of it, for caseworkers do not tattle and will not scold. The caseworker must be ready to interpret to the foster mother what is implied when the child is being his most aggravating, acting out his fear and his resentment, or when he is testing his new security with her. The caseworker must talk over and over and over again with the own parents, searching always for some strength in the home on which can be built a rehabilitation that will make a return of the child possible. He must interpret to the school that sees the child every day, to boys' clubs or girls' clubs that may offer the badly needed group therapy, to private organizations that may possibly furnish special treats for the foster child, to the general tax-paying public that foots most of the bills and that often is highly verbal about "welfare kids" who get dental care they cannot afford for their own children.

CHAPTER XII

The adolescent

ADOLESCENCE is a physical phenomenon that occurs with the changing glandular development of puberty. Biological maturation brings awakening sexual interests, and psychological maturation brings strong pressure to be free of earlier infancy dependence. Adolescence is a territory that must be crossed by everyone who travels the road from childhood to maturity, and for some the way is rough. How rough it is for any adolescent depends on his own psychological and emotional constitution and on the amount of help and understanding he gets from his family, his school, his environment in general.

Each adolescent must face and accomplish four tasks. He must emancipate himself from parental authority and strike out for himself, acquiring judgment to make his own decisions. He must learn to accept heterosexual life in preparation for the responsibilities of a later marital relationship. He must find the vocation that is right for him and prepare himself for it. And he must grow out of the narrowness of childish self-interest, integrating altruism into his personality and broadening his sympathy to include as much of humanity as his experiences can fit him to understand. A failure in any one of these tasks will make a complete and satisfactory maturity impossible. Watching the adolescent as he struggles, experiments, makes false starts only to back up and try again, can be a harrowing experience for anyone whose life is closely involved with his— his parents, for example.

At best, the effort of a youngster to strike out for himself involves a rugged time for his parents. As the child leaves the shelter of the family and begins to identify with his own age group, the dismayed parents may find themselves watching behavior that would have been far from acceptable in their young days. Bobby-soxers insist on doing what all the other teenagers do whether or not the activity meets family standards. The girls wear tight levis to the movies instead of skirts, and they wear the shortest of shorts on the street. Boys demand the right to drive the family car. And they all want to date at an age much younger than was considered suitable a generation ago. This, of course, is all part of the normal picture. A generation ago teenagers were demanding something else that shocked the parents of that day, and the children of those who are today's adolescents will in their time go through a similar healthy revolt. Any adolescent has to try his wings and prove his independence to himself. He wants to tackle new enterprises without advice or assistance. At the same time, he desperately needs the reassurance that he has someone back of him if things go wrong. He demands the rights of an adult and the privileges of a child. For the best of parents it is a trying time. They are in turn exasperated, worried, deeply hurt, and then baffled by the unexpected childishness and dependence of a gawky son who yesterday would not listen to a word of advice.

Sometimes parents cling to the feeling of adult superiority they have enjoyed while the children were small. Without being aware of what they are doing, they may act to prolong their own pleasure in authority by blocking their child's freedom and independence. Or they may feel sincerely apprehensive of what may happen if their child is left without adult direction. They cannot trust the judgment of a teenager who only yesterday was their bumbling infant. There is some reality to this fear. Adolescents can make serious blunders as they try out their experiments in independence. They can land the family car upside down in a ditch, or elope with the wrong mate, or involve themselves with the law. It demands a great deal of self-control to leave the youngsters free for their trial flights, and a delicate judgment to know when to step in to prevent real disaster. This is the time when groups are most valuable. Church groups, school organizations, community activities directed by an understanding leader, can satisfy the adolescent urge for activities performed in common with others of his own age and at the same time provide acceptable leadership that assures safety.

There are adolescents who find this step toward independence exceedingly difficult. Instead of tackling the wild and dangerous experimentation that attracts his friends, a teenager may stay close to home, acquiescent and conforming. Sometimes parents and school authorities regard this untroublesome youngster with satisfaction and admiration, but they are wrong to do so. A too-conforming adolescent will not develop into an independent adult. It is unfortunate for small children to be overprotected by their parents. An individual who has not been permitted normal contact with the reality of competition, of criticism, of possible failure, while he is still a child is very likely, when he is an adolescent, to be afraid to risk leaving the security which his home has always provided and strike out alone. Then we find a boy who has graduated from high school but is reluctant to leave for college or to assume his own place in the business world, or a girl unable to give up the shelter of her mother's home to make a home for herself and her husband and her own children. Here again the group leader can help. With encouragement such a timid teenager may take a few tentative steps, and if no harm follows, may gradually discover the pleasures of independence. The important thing is for grown-ups to see the danger of too much conformity to adult direction. They should not be too much pleased by this conformity even if it does make life easier for the adults and temporarily safer for the adolescent.

At the same time that the healthy teenager is seeking independence, a growing interest in heterosexual activity is resulting in a normal if frequently a somewhat unpleasant rejection of the parent of the same sex. Daughters are rudely critical of mother's taste in make-up, her social activities, her speech, her housekeeping standards. Sons reject all advice from their fathers, call them "old fogies," or "squares," or whatever the current phrase of disapprobation may be. Yet a need for security remains, since the teenager is still half a child, and this leads to an acceptance by the adolescent of a "parent substitute" who is in a position to provide security without exerting the authority of a real parent. Hence the typical idolization of an adult of the same sex. Schoolgirl crushes and a boy's imitation of the mannerisms of an athletic coach are normal. They can be safeguards if the right idol is selected and a serious danger if the wrong one is picked. It is to be hoped that the youngster's environment, his church, his school, his neighborhood, can provide a model that will be constructive rather than damaging.

Simultaneously, the emotionally healthy adolescent is unconsciously adjusting himself to a heterosexual relationship. This means dating. It means an effort to satisfy curiosity about the opposite sex and about sexual activities. That it might also involve experimentation is not surprising in view of the strong stimulation which the adolescent encounters on every side, from movies, television programs, fiction, popular songs and singers, advertisements which emphasize the social stigma of any failure to allure the opposite sex. The adults who want to help an adolescent cannot afford to be merely critical and judgmental. The world is what it is, and there is little point in attempting to shut our youngsters away from the stimulation it thrusts upon them. The only thing to do is to try to provide activities which will give an adolescent an opportunity to work off excess energy in constructive ways, such as sports, chaperoned parties, club work, and to satisfy their curiosity with facts straightforwardly presented. The hope is that good early standards have been strongly enough instilled to carry youth over "Fool's Hill" without stumbling.

Another task which the adolescent has to face is the selection of a suitable vocation, and to do this wisely everyone—parents, teachers, guidance directors, the youngster himself—must hold firmly to reality. This is not easy. Adults have trouble seeing themselves as they really are, free from wishful thinking. It is no wonder that adolescents, untried and inexperienced, visualize themselves in all sorts of romantic and exciting roles for which they may be utterly unsuited. Girls yearn to be movie actresses or highly paid fashion models whether or not they have the talent or physical equipment for such careers. Boys want to be space pilots without stopping to think that such jobs involve high skills in mathematics, which the average schoolboy loathes. Girls plan to be nurses without remembering about bedpans and blood. Boys decide to be policemen and never think of the miles of pavement to be tramped, the hours of traffic duty. Usually, however, a clear and explicit description of what the glamorous jobs entail can bring an adolescent down to solid earth.

It is even more dangerous when a parent has unsuitable ambitions for a youngster. A father visualizes his son as an athletic hero in the college where he was once a shining light, or a mother plans a career for her daughter that will compensate for the career she herself sacrificed when she married. This may present a real and very serious obstacle in the way of the youngster's adjustment in life. Even if he has achieved emancipation from his parents in most areas, still, if he has been presented from earliest childhood with one single goal, that ideal may be so firmly incorporated into his unconscious portrait of himself that any failure to reach it may be a death blow to his self-esteem, leaving him convinced of his own worthlessness.

Any plan for a life occupation must be based, not on wishful thinking, not on any unrealistic notion of the fun of being a cowboy or an actress or what not, not on what father hopes for his son or mother for her daughter, but on the youngster's own individual tastes, on his intellectual capacity, his physical stamina, his special skills and abilities, and it must take into account his limitations, physical, mental, and emotional. Any teacher, guidance counselor, or group leader who observes an adolescent struggling futilely to achieve a goal for which he is unsuited, has a casework job on his hands. Whether the youngster is heading in the wrong direction because of his mistaken notion of what the chosen career involves, or because of his inability to accept his own limitations, or because of a pathetic effort to live up to some impossible ideal set up by his parents, whatever the reason, the youngster needs realistic clarification of the job he has selected and the preparations required for it. Possibly he will need some interpretation of why he is trying for this particular unsuitable goal. If the shift in direction involves, or seems to the adolescent to involve, hauling down of his banner, he will also need a strong relationship with an adult who can give him emotional support and, quite probably, help to manipulate his environment so that suitable educational or training opportunities will be opened to him and he can enter a more appropriate vocation.

A word of warning. Before the worker starts to make suggestions or give advice to an adolescent, he must make very sure indeed that his diagnosis of the youngster's capacities is based on a *complete* and accurate knowledge of all the pertinent facts. Remember the girl mentioned in Chapter VI whose life came so close to being spoiled because a faculty advisor failed to realize that her abilities were temporarily in abeyance because of a physical condition that was corrected under medication within a few weeks. Also, sometimes a strong emotional drive can carry an individual through to success in spite of obstacles that seem unsurmountable to the onlooker. This has been true of many persons afflicted with what have seemed to be crippling physical disabilities. The degree of emotional drive must be taken into consideration by the caseworker as he makes his diagnosis.

The fourth task faced by all adolescents is that of growing out of the self-interest of childhood into the broader, more altruistic interests of the mature individual. At first a small child is interested only in what happens to himself. His concern gradually widens to include his parents, his brothers and sisters, then other relatives, his playmates, his school chums, eventually his townspeople, or at least those among them who belong to the same religious faith or social stratum, or business group. We have all known adults whose altruistic development halted at the stage of childhood. The psychopathic individuals described in Chapter VII never got beyond the infant phase of self-interest. The majority, however, include in their concern people who are like themselves, with similar background and interests. A few great ones have been able to identify with the entire human race, feeling joy or pain with all humanity. This span of altruistic interest widens with experience. A child cannot be expected to identify with a type of person he has never known and cannot imagine. We have all seen the exquisite discomfort of a foreign child when he is first introduced into a school where foreign-born people are seldom seen, where the native children have had no opportunity to develop an awareness that covers youngsters of different appearance and strange speech. An adult whose circumstances have held him in one narrow groove, social, geographical, educational, or emotional, cannot immediately identify with a person of widely different background. Experience will widen interests through actual contact with different sorts of people, or the identification may come vicariously through reading. Adolescence is the period when this interest has its most rapid expansion, and anything which the family, the educator, or the caseworker can do to provide stimulation for this expansion will be a valuable help toward maturation. Books, discussion groups, debating clubs, all may stir the imagination. Some communities organize groups of young people for volunteer social service, such as helping a discouraged, overworked young mother redecorate her dingy house, collecting used furniture for a family who have been burned out of their home, helping out in a playground to keep small children safely occupied while their mother does her shopping or takes a much needed rest, entertaining in nursing homes or institutions for the aged. Anything that provides a glimpse of how the other nine tenths live will help to stimulate the imagination, broaden the sympathies, and give the adolescent a better foundation for his own approaching maturity.

Clearly, an adolescent runs the risk of failing in any or all of the tasks he faces during this period of his life. If his family has overprotected him throughout his childhood, he will find it difficult if not impossible to set out on any independent enterprise unsupported by his parents. If, on the other hand, his parents have rejected him either covertly or openly, he may very well be impelled to turn with some violence against the standards set up for him; or, if his home has never provided him with consistent standards he may, in his groping after some satisfying identification with his peers, attach himself to the wrong groups. Defiance of traffic rules, thefts of cars, breaking into stores, threats of violence against school authorities, destruction of property, all phases of the Blackboard Jungle behavior, are prompted partly by reaction against adult control and partly by a strong identification with a gang of his own age which can swing the youngster along with increasing momentum in whatever direction a wrong-headed mob happens to take.

Obviously, delinquent behavior must be controlled, both for the protection of the public and for the safeguarding of the young person's future. Sometimes the only immediately available control is custodial care in an institution, and if the institution is wisely managed, it may provide exactly what the adolescent most needs—a chance to relate to an adult whose standard of behavior is socially acceptable. Through this relationship, if it is a strong one, the damaged conscience of the youngster can be rebuilt. Institutional life for the adolescent also offers an opportunity for him to be "one of the gang," or, in more professional terms, for "peer identification with a group performing under wise direction." Since this is the period in a young person's life when belonging to a group is so very important, this opportunity is good. However, unhappily, the right institution is not always available, or it is so overcrowded that no productive program is possible. Then the best that can be expected of such placement is temporary custodial care—and release in a couple of years of an adolescent who is bitter, resentful, and probably aware of a number of antisocial tricks he did not know before he went in.

Often, placement of a predelinquent adolescent in a foster home is more beneficial than institutional placement. It is certainly preferable to commitment to an overcrowded or poorly run institution. If the foster parents understand adolescent problems, and if they are strong and at the same time warm and accepting, they may well be able to fill the youngster's emotional needs so that he has no further compulsion to act out resentment or fear. Such a substitute home may provide a standard of behavior which the child will accept if he has not been too seriously damaged before he enters the new experience. Such foster homes are not too easy to find, however, and if neither foster home nor institution is available, then it is the responsibility of some worker in the school or the church or the community house or the local boys' or girls' club to do what can be done. But it is uphill work while the young person is still in daily contact with the home which failed him in the first place, and with the gang that started him off in the wrong direction.

Fortunately for teachers, parents, group workers, and the future of the human race, by far the largest proportion of our adolescents come through their time of storm and stress with all flags flying, even though the others do get the loudest publicity. However, even for the best of them there will be difficult moods. The adolescent does not draw breath who has not at one time or another been furiously angry and resentful of parental restrictions. Many of them assume intermittently a don't-give-a-damn attitude most trying to adults but necessary to the youngster who feels he must hide his miserable fear of personal inadequacy. Obviously, adolescent behavior must be held within the bounds of public safety, but within those limits the teenager must experiment and try out his strength and learn for himself what he can do and what he cannot without inviting dire consequences. And throughout this whole adolescent period he yearns to be treated as a person, an individual in his own right.

During these trying years it helps any adolescent to be given an opportunity to express his angers, his hopes, his self-doubts to someone who accepts him as an individual, who does not sneer at his callow, groping philosophies, who does not look shocked at his aggressions and revolts, who is not scornful of his taste in music, his style of dancing, his aspirations. But mostly it helps to be able to pour out anger and resentment without bringing down wrath on his head. Foster parents at the end of their patience have been known to call the child placing agency to say in despair that they cannot stand sixteen-year-old Johnny another minute, and will the caseworker please come and give him what-for. The worker goes, takes Johnny for a ride in the agency car, maybe buys him a coke, listens without any suggestion of disapproval while he sputters about all the things wrong with the school, the foster home, and his life. The worker says he will see him again in a couple days, and takes him home again. The foster mother calls up the agency to report that Johnny is fine—what magic did the caseworker use? But the only magic was acceptance and an ability to listen. Rage and resentment are healthier out than in, and it is better to talk them out than to slug them out.

CHAPTER XIII

The retarded child

THERE ARE a great many facets to the problem presented by the mentally retarded child. For most children their own home is the place where their emotional needs can be met in the most satisfactory way. That is where children ought to be able to count on finding love, security, assurance of being wanted. However, as we have seen, this is unhappily not always true even for normal children, and for the retarded or atypical child there is a considerable possibility that home may not be the right place for him. There are questions to be answered before we can know.

How much rough treatment will a retarded child be obliged to take from other children on the block? Is the school equipped to help at all in his training and education, or are the teachers overworked, underpaid, and strongly inhospitable to the idea of accepting an atypical child in the crowded classroom? Most important of all, how do the parents themselves really feel about their child, and how capable are they of working through their inevitable disappointment without too much stress within themselves and without unconscious punishment of the child? The answers to these questions depend on the neighbors, the family, the school, and on the type and seriousness of the retardation.

Mental retardation ranges all the way from the barely perceptible slowness of a child who must struggle with his schoolwork but who can, under direction, work quite well with his hands, to the gross retardation of a child who can never be toilet trained, can never walk or talk, but will remain forever on the level of a three- or four-month-old infant. The causes of retardation are varied. Brain damage may be caused by birth injury, by an insufficient supply of oxygen during the birth process, by accident or by disease after birth. It may come from pressure on the brain, as from a tumor or a hydrocephalic condition, or it may be the result of a glandular imbalance, such as hypothyroidism, which can slow down anybody's mental activity, or a pituitary lack which halts all development. Damage to the fetus in the mother's womb is now believed to be the cause of the Mongoloid type of retardation. Some conditions which resemble mental retardation are actually caused by emotional blocks and can be corrected when the source of the emotional difficulty is removed. The physical basis of some retardations can be corrected. Tumors may be amenable to surgery. Glandular imbalances yield to medication. A child who is hard of hearing or who has a visual handicap may seem dull and unresponsive although there is nothing whatever wrong with his mind once access to it is established.

Some types of mental retardation can never be corrected or improved. Nevertheless, the afflicted child must have physical comfort and emotional security, and he must be given the opportunity to develop to the limit of his capacity. A decision must be made as to the environment where this can best be secured, but often a number of factors enter the situation which make a realistic plan difficult to carry through.

Sometimes retardation is not apparent, at least to the layman, until the child starts school, but often a doctor knows as soon as an infant is born that brain damage exists. This is true, for example, of the Mongoloid type, in which the stigmata are evident at birth. A physician in these cases will usually tell the parents at once what they have to face. Now let us see what happens to the mother when she gives birth to a child recognized at once as atypical.

She has spent nine months looking forward to her baby's arrival, planning for him, gathering clothes and equipment, perhaps preparing a special room for the nursery. All her friends have known of her pregnancy, have looked forward with her. Quite probably there have been a few stork showers. The expectant father has planned too. Maybe he has already bought a baseball and bat, or submitted the child's name for admission at his favorite preparatory school. Then, before the mother leaves the hospital, she and her husband are told by the doctor that their child is not normal. In some ways this knowledge is a more severe shock to the parents than the death of the baby might be. Quite possibly the doctor recommends that the infant not be taken home, but placed directly from the hospital in an institution which specializes in the care of such children. Probably the parents, stunned by the magnitude of their disaster, are unable to decide at once what they want to do. Perhaps the mother goes home without the baby, leaving him in the hospital until she can think things through clearly. At this point the doctor often refers the family for casework help, either to the hospital's own social service department, or to an agency in the community, or he may ask the priest or the pastor or a family friend to give some support. The helping person, whoever he is, must then be prepared for what is happening within the mother's personality and for the contradictory pressures that will be brought to bear from the community.

Almost certainly the parents will be deluged with sympathy and advice, well meant but not too helpful and not well informed. The sympathy can be debilitating, and the advice is sure to be confusing. The unhappy parents will be told that doctors do not always know —the baby looks all right, maybe there is nothing wrong with him. Why not just ignore what he has said and wait to see what happens when the child grows older? This may mean hope deferred, and more bitter disappointment later. They will be told that institutions are dirty, neglectful, downright abusive, that they charge exorbitant fees and then let the children die for lack of proper care. They will be told harrowing though apocryphal tales of such occurrences. On the other hand, they will be told that institutionalization is the only way for such a child to have adequate care and a chance to make social contacts with others like himself as he grows older. They will be told that only the most monstrous parents could dream of dumping their child in an institution, and half an hour later someone will point out how criminal it would be to subject themselves and any other children they may have to a life revolving around the demands of a mental defective. Someone is sure to say that what has happened is God's will and they should bow under the yoke. They will also be told that feeblemindedness is inherited and there must be something in their family background to account for its appearance. They will be strongly advised, possibly by the family doctor, to forget this child as quickly as possible so that they can have a normal family life.

At the same time that all these confusing contradictions are being hurled at them from outside, things are happening to their inner selves. Deep disappointment, grief, perhaps bitterness—these emotions are inevitable and probably obvious to anyone who knows them. But there is something else which only a psychiatrist or a trained caseworker might anticipate, and that is the powerful though subconscious and quite illogical feeling of guilt which so often in such cases distorts the parents' thinking. If there is in them, as there is in so many of us, any subterranean river of guilt, it will swell now to a most powerful flood, able to sweep all before it. It may never emerge to the surface of their thinking, nor be accepted by their conscious mind, but if it *is* there, it will surely influence their behavior during the ensuing months, and perhaps for years to come.

An individual may go through all his life comfortably unaware that he has any neurotic tendencies. If things go well for him, he may never have occasion to find out. But for each of us there is a breaking point when we can no longer face life without the protection of some sort of defense between us and naked reality. That point may well be reached by a woman when she learns she has given birth to a defective baby. She may have been self-confident, happy, and assured all her life, and now, suddenly faced with this tragedy out of her own womb, she feels impelled to throw herself into the care of this defective child in atonement for a sin she cannot explain to her conscious mind. There may be no reality whatever to account for the conviction of sin, but the urge to atone is often very powerful, and the woman's inability to explain the urge does not lessen it.

Like all neuroses, this one cannot be touched by logic. The mother may or may not be able to verbalize a rationalization of the feeling which possesses her. She may call it mother love, or pity for the infant, or she may be able to say "I must take care of him to make up." She does not say make up for what. She does not know, but she feels she must do it. This subconscious urge, unfortunately, is often strengthened by the tales she hears about the horrors of institutions, and by the preachments thrown at her about God's will and the duty of parenthood. Whether she can work this through and, with her husband, make a plan based on reality depends on her own native ego strength and on the degree of support she gets from her caseworker, professional or lay.

However, the retardation may not be the sort that is evident at once. The parents take their baby home in pride from the hospital, with no suspicion that anything is wrong with him—until he should begin to walk and does not, or should start talking and fails to do so, or perhaps not until he is unable to do first grade work in school and behaves like a little demon in class because of his frustration and sense of failure. A slowly awakened awareness of their child's deficiency may present even more psychological and emotional problems than if the parents had known the situation at once. Almost always there must be months, even years, of repeated tests and examinations, of uncertainty, of hope that is disappointed again and again. There is always a need for expert medical opinions in case surgery or medication could correct the condition. But when at the end of all tests the parents must face the inescapable fact of their child's mental deficiency, and must make plans around it, then they will be beset by the same confusions of contradictory advice from neighbors, the same turmoil of inner conflicts that the parents encountered who knew at once of their baby's condition. These parents, too, will need casework help to enable them to think honestly and to plan realistically.

What the worker must remember and somehow convey to the parents is that there are good institutions and bad ones. Some are expensive, some adjust their fees to the ability of the parents to pay. In most states there are state schools for the care and training of the mentally retarded, and these state schools expect no more in payment than the family can give. In some states such schools are overcrowded. In some communities a retarded child would be accepted and absorbed into the group with no embarrassment. In others, the life of a retarded child would be made miserable. He would be the butt of cruel jokes from children, pushed aside, left out of everything. A retarded child, like every other child, needs the companionship of his peers by the time he reaches eight or nine, and if he is not to have it in the community in which his parents live, then quite possibly he would be happier in a school with others like himself who offer no serious competition.

All that caseworkers can do for parents of a retarded child is to help them get at the facts of the retardation, and then to explore the resources, study with them the attitudes of the neighborhood and the schools, and give the mother all possible support as she tries to work through any need she may feel to punish herself. Only if these things have been done can any plan for the child be made with a solid basis in reality instead of in superstition, sentimentality, or a guilt neurosis.

The final decisions must rest on such realistic factors as the availability of good institutions, whether this particular child could benefit more from the training and social life offered in the institution or from the security of life in his own family, how much suffering might be inflicted on other members of the family if the child remains, how much rejection the child would have to endure from an unsympathetic community or from his own self-punishing family.

The caseworker must be prepared to give a strong supportive relationship as the mother resolves any possible neurotic guilt feelings she may have. He must have an intimate knowledge of the resources available for the atypical child, and be ready to help the parents make up their minds as to what plan is the best for their child.

Probably the most difficult situation of all is the one in which a mentally retarded child is born into a home where the parents themselves are mentally dull. If the child has inherited a familial type of retardation, all the troubles found in a normal home are aggravated by the parents' inability to provide good training or adequate control at home, and probably by their blindness to the disadvantage of allowing such a child complete freedom, especially after he or she approaches puberty. A worker has to determine at what point he is justified in using the pressures which all his training has impressed on him he should seldom if ever use. Should he postpone action until the child gets into really serious trouble so that the court must intervene with the weight of authority? Or, aware of what the parents do not realize, should he forget the tenets he has been taught of individual choice for the client, and insist on placement of the child in an institution before trouble starts? Will the unfortunate child be more damaged by the loss of security with his own family, or by the lack of training and control which a specializing institution can supply?

Questions like these are posers, and there is no easy way to answer them. One can only rely on an honest study of each individual situation.

CHAPTER XIV

The physically handicapped

ANYONE who tries to help a handicapped person, or that person's family, should always work under the direction of a physician or a medical social worker. Any plan for change of environment, for recreation, employment, occupational therapy, must be approved by someone thoroughly acquainted with the medical problems of the client. Once medical clearance is obtained, the caseworker proceeds as with any other client, keeping always in the forefront of his mind the fact that the handicapped person is first of all a person and that the handicap is secondary. The handicap, to be sure, is a reality which limits activity and probably influences attitudes. But the person is an individual and as such is different from all other handicapped persons even if the handicaps are the same.

In a ward of ten amputees there will be no two with precisely the same attitude toward what has happened to them. The differences will depend on the individual's age, on how the amputation occurred, on previous plans and ambitions, on early training or education, on the degree of ingrained stoicism, on the extent of emotional support offered by each man's family, on any number of other factors. One may be crushed and withdrawn, ready to give up thinking about any further life for himself; another may be angry and resentful, in need of an opportunity to express his bitterness; another may have accepted his fate and be prepared, with help, to make practical plans for his future. Still another may even be secretly relieved that he has been removed from the struggle of competition, content to be taken care of by nurse or wife or mother. It is quite possible that none of them can verbalize his attitude, but the caseworker must be alert to the personality differences that exist, to the individualities. A case load, all of whom are receiving Aid to the Disabled through the public assistance program, is not to be thought of as a uniform group of cases in a given category. Each one is equally separate and individual. Patients in a rehabilitation center, children in a convalescent home, a blind baby, a deaf adolescent— all are people. This is sometimes easy to forget, especially if the nurse, the occupational therapist, the caseworker, has too much to do. All the blind must live in the dark; all the deaf, in silence. All the patients with similar polio handicaps need similar exercises. But each one has his own private feelings about his handicap and about his life.

Even the parents of the handicapped person may forget this. The disaster of the handicap itself is so crushing that the family may be able to think of nothing but the handicap or the effect it may have on them as a family. A wife may be overwhelmed by her own emotions when she first learns that her husband will never walk again. A mother may be swept beyond coherent thought when she is told that her baby is blind.

In fact, the psychological and emotional problems faced by the parents of a physically handicapped child are not unlike those faced by the parents of the mentally retarded. There is a probability that the parents will have to live through a time of agonizing suspense while they turn from one medical advisor to another, hoping that the condition can be ameliorated if not corrected. Money and time and energy and hope will be flung into what may turn out to be a bottomless pit. Then, when the parents must face the realization that the handicap will inevitably be of long duration, or even permanent, there is a possibility that they will go through a period of asking Fate bitterly: "Why did this have to happen to us?" It is quite natural that there should be moments of resentment when the parents think of the money and the time and energy that must go into the care and training of a handicapped child, perhaps while other members of the family are deprived of education or opportunities. Also, it must not be forgotten that some handicaps induce a deep-seated shame in the parents. This is especially true if the handicap is obvious, or if the condition entails some abnormal physical motion, as in cerebral palsy, or the possibility of a public seizure, as in epilepsy. There is likewise, as with the family of a retarded child, the strong possibility that there may be a subconscious conviction of guilt, a feeling that they, the parents, must somehow be to blame, and that they are being punished for a forgotten sin.

Sometimes the resentment and shame are overt, resulting in physical neglect of the child. Then we find a blind child, or a spastic, left to crouch untended in a corner. More often, the resentment is strongly repressed, inducing a "reaction formation," that is, an unhealthy overemphasis on the opposite feeling. Then we find the parents who overprotect the handicapped child, punishing themselves by waiting on him far more than is necessary or even desirable. It has even happened that such self-punishing parents, unable to delegate any part of their self-imposed duty, refuse to permit the child to leave home for medical treatment or special training even when all logic should inform them that such treatment and training could provide a more nearly normal life for their child and for them.

A caseworker, acquainted by training and experience with the handicapped child's special needs, is likely to be vividly aware of those needs but to see much less clearly the motivation of the parents' resistance to separation. This is not strange, for the parents themselves are not consciously aware of it, and will present confusing rationalizations: "My child is such a baby still. I can't let him go away from me." Or, "He depends on me. He'll cry his poor eyes out if I'm not right there every minute." Or, "What would people say if I put my child away in some cold, impersonal institution?" Or, "This is the cross I have to bear. It is the Lord's will." Or, "I would die of worry if I let anyone else take care of my child."

Not one of these attitudes provides a wholesome climate for a child, as any caseworker knows. But they are impervious to logic, as are all neurotic reactions. Perhaps skilled psychiatry could uncover the conviction of sin that has its inadequate basis in some childish naughtiness of years ago, and by bringing it to the light of adult awareness minimize the unconscious impulse to atone; but no caseworker, no layman, should ever dive into such deep waters. The caseworker, understanding even when he cannot correct the neurosis, must not be impatient or critical or judgmental. He might suggest psychiatric therapy if it is available and if he believes the family will accept it, but his most valuable contribution will be in the area of external realities. He must keep his feet solidly on the ground, maintain his contact on a factual level, talk about what the child needs in medication, surgery, education, training. He must first discuss what can be supplied by the parents at home and move only gradually to needs that must be met away from home. He may give direct help to the child if he has the medical training to do this, and he must offer the mother a strong support, not necessarily for what she is actually doing for the child but to the confused, unhappy, guilty person groping behind her rationalizations. It may happen that such a sympathetic support will in time bring the mother to an acceptance of the child's reality needs and make it possible to plan with her toward treatment of the child away from home.

Sometimes talking about other mothers of handicapped children will give a mother the realization that her situation is not unlike that endured by other people. Her child is not wholly strange and different. Other children have similar handicaps—or even worse ones. She is not set apart from other mothers, doing solitary penance. Other women face the same problems. Sometimes a visit to a child's hospital, or group work with mothers of handicapped children, will help her toward reality and acceptance of a plan which provides for expert medical help or physical therapy or specialized training by someone better equipped than she is.

We have been speaking as though all handicapped children should leave home and all mothers of handicapped children raise unreasonable objections. Neither is true. Many mothers have faced their problem squarely and realistically and want nothing more than information about existing facilities for help, and assistance in reaching them. Moreover, it is by no means always necessary or desirable for a handicapped child to leave home. The decision must depend on the resources of the home and of the community as well as on the type and extent of the handicap. But whatever plan is arrived at, it must, to be of use to the child, be based on reality. And sometimes the parents' disturbed emotionalism is the first hurdle the caseworker meets.

When a caseworker is working directly with a handicapped child he will do well to remember that probably the greatest hazard the child has to meet is the hazard of pity. It is all too easy for a youngster hampered by braces to accept the help of sympathetic adults when he should be learning to get about by himself. The debilitating pleasure of overdependence can ruin the child's chances of any normal personality development and may retard his physical development too if it prevents him from exercising his weakened muscles. This applies to adults as well as children. Remember Mr. Kelso, who was a nuisance to himself and to his wife while he let himself be waited on but whose personality improved when he found the pleasure of recognition and accomplishment through doing something for himself and for others.

Speaking of direct work with a handicapped child, Louise Raymond says:

He needs to learn two things: first, to accept his disability; and second, to be independent in spite of it. In order to help him, you will want never to seem to ignore the handicap, to act as if it were non-existent. It is there. He knows it and he is aware that everyone else knows it. Be matter-of-fact about it. You wouldn't try to hush up bright red hair if he had it. So there's no reason either to avert your eyes when you see him trying to get his braces through his trouser leg or to rush over and say pityingly, "Oh, it's too hard! Mommy will do it for you." Just say matter-of-factly, "The brace catches doesn't it? Here, I'll help you." Show him how to keep it from catching, and help him until he can do it alone. Let him do everything that he can and wants to unless it is downright dangerous. At the same time you will want to help him accept the fact that there will always be some things he can't do without so much effort that it really isn't worth while to try. Learning to do necessary things, yes—even if it's painful and tedious. But try to stop him from feeling that just *because* of his handicap he must learn to do everything his unhandicapped friends do and do it better. You want to help him to live in peace with the concrete fact that he can't, that in many instances he must find something altogether different in the line of special accomplishment. Perhaps if, as so often happens, he has a compensating talent, you can help him find it. It will do wonders for him to become known as "the boy who does the magic tricks" instead of "that lame kid." [1]

One of the conditions most likely to leave an inexperienced worker feeling futile and embarrassed is blindness. The first time he faces an unhappy mother of a blind child, he may not know at all how to help her help the child. However, if she has resolved her own personal feelings about the condition and is ready now to accept suggestions of what to do and how to do it, there are some practical recommendations to make.

First of all, blindness is not the most important thing about the child. He is a child with the same impulses as other children, the same need for emotional security, for reassurance that he is loved and wanted. But to a blind child a smile from across the room has no meaning. A blind baby should be talked to and handled more than other babies, since his only contact with the world outside himself comes through hearing and touch. The mother must be prepared for the fact that a blind baby will be slower to do most things than his sighted brother. This does not indicate mental slowness but simply the fact that he cannot imitate facial expressions, or patty-cake, or peekaboo, or waving good-by. He may never creep at all, or he may creep backward—very sensible, too, since creeping forward puts his head in a vulnerable position to bump things he cannot see to avoid. Bottoms can absorb bumps better than heads. He may be slow to walk—after all, so far as he knows, he has no place to go. It may take a lot of encouragement to get him started. Letting him stand on his mother's feet while she supports him by the hands and moves forward with tiny steps may give him the idea of walking. Unlike the sighted baby, he cannot be lured into lurching from one adult to another as they hold out inviting arms. Rather, he must be called, by a voice he recognizes, and the distance between him and the adult must be shorter than for his sighted sister. He cannot orient himself by looking around the room. He can do it only by touch—the feel of the bare floor or of a rug under his feet, the sofa or the chair on which he supports himself—but first he must get to the floor or the rug or the sofa. Things about the house

---

[1] Raymond, *Adoption and After,* p. 149.

that make sounds will help give a concept of distance—a canary singing in the dining room, glass bells lightly jingling in a breeze from the open front door. Sometimes there might be very low music in the living room, but radio or television programs must not be going on all the time. The sounds are too confusing to a blind person, child or adult.

A blind child should be allowed to touch everything, even at the cost of some breakage. His toys should provide a variety of textures, plastic and fur and wool. They should help him learn about shapes, round, flat, and square. Identification is more easily established if they have sound. Toys that ring or rattle or bang are fine. A blind child must learn about stairs, and the yard outside, and swings, and jungle gyms, and sidewalks, and curbs. The mother of a blind child must be braced to let him try things for himself, accepting his bumps, and at the same time she must be unobtrusively alert to keep him away from real dangers such as fire and boiling water and traffic. Unfortunately, it is usually easier for a mother to guard her child from danger than it is for her to remember how important it is for him to experiment and learn about his world in the only way he can.

When a blind child reaches school age it may be the responsibility of the caseworker to learn what resources are available. There are in most states residential schools for blind children that start with kindergarten and continue through high school courses and perhaps even into vocational training. But if he attends a residential school the blind child must go away from home, which may or may not be the best plan, depending on the sort of home it is, the maturity or immaturity of the child, and what might be available in the immediate community. Some public schools are hospitable to the acceptance of a blind child in the regular class. Perhaps he studies part of the time with the classroom teacher and part of the time with a special instructor assigned to work with blind children throughout the school system. In some areas an itinerant teacher may be available to visit the schools, help blind students directly, and assist the regular teacher with suggestions. Any school can secure special equipment for teaching the blind, including books in Braille and talking books. However, some schools, especially in rural areas, may not have the resources of special teachers, and the authorities may then feel unequipped to further the education of a blind child in any way.

Sometimes the caseworker must do some "missionary work" with the authorities so that they will comprehend a blind child's capacity to learn and to do and appreciate his need for normal companionship.

The lack of companionship may, in fact, be a serious problem in the development of a blind child, especially if he is an only child in an isolated rural home. The chance to be with normal, sighted children of his own age is one of the advantages of the public school system for a blind child. True, in a residential school he would get specialized training, but he would have no opportunity to mingle with the sighted as he must do sooner or later in his life. Another advantage, of course, is that if he remains in his own community he will have a normal home life with his own family. The advantages and the disadvantages of each plan must be carefully considered by the child's family and by the caseworker. The weight will vary in each situation.

There are a few pointers that a worker will find useful when dealing with a blind adult. First, be as natural as possible. A blind girl once said that she spent the first twenty minutes following a new introduction in putting the sighted person at ease. Do not try to avoid using words such as "look" or "see." They are a normal part of a sighted person's vocabulary, and it would be awkward and strained to dodge their use. When leading a blind person one should not clutch his arm; he will take his companion's arm and walk slightly behind him. In that way the blind person can follow easily the motion of the other person's body, turning as he turns, knowing in time that there is a curb or a step. Taking his arm removes the blind person's body from shoulder contact, and also puts his arm in a clumsy, uncomfortable position when a guide attempts to help him up a step by lifting on his elbow. Tell him when friends are approaching, and mention it if an acquaintance waves from across the street. If one enters a room with him, that person should tell him who is in the room, or speak to the others by name to give him a clue. On entering a room where a blind person is already present, tell him who you are when you speak to him. Most blind people have developed an excellent memory for voices, but it is easier to be able to say, "Yes, I recognized your voice right away" than it is to try to conceal a failure to know the speaker while he guesses his identity. When guiding a blind person to a chair, place him in front of it so that he touches it with the back of his knees and give him, if it can be done tactfully, some idea of whether it is an armchair, a folding wooden chair, a low-seated chair. It must be disconcerting to find oneself dropping nine inches further than one is prepared for, even if one lands eventually on soft upholstery. When one eats for the first time with a blind person one should ask him whether he wants help in cutting meat or pouring cream into his coffee. He will probably say frankly what he can do for himself and what he would like help in doing. Be sure that each article he is to use stands apart from every other article. A glass of water can be pulled over if it is resting on the edge of the linen when the blind man picks up his napkin. He can be helped to locate articles by a description of their position as though his plate were the face of a clock: "Potato at three o'clock; meat at twelve. There's a bit of jelly just about to slide off at nine o'clock."

Waiters are sometimes inclined to treat a blind person as though he were also deaf and dumb and feebleminded. "Would your friend like soup or fruit cup?" they will ask. Sometimes this can be avoided if the sighted person reads the menu to his companion before the waiter arrives for the order. Most blind persons have of necessity acquired superb memories and will be able to keep the items in mind better than the average person. In any case, even if the waiter asks such silly questions, let the blind man answer for himself.

Successful casework with the blind, or with those handicapped in any other fashion, requires imagination. A worker should envision not only how he would feel if he had the handicap, for certainly the handicap will not be the only difference between client and worker, but think what *he* would want, how *he* would feel, if *he* had the handicap, and the handicapped person's background, and temperament, and training and education and skill and ambition and expectation, the client's childhood experiences and adult hopes. That is empathy, and empathy is something caseworkers need.

CHAPTER XV

The unmarried mother

WHEN a pregnant, unmarried girl in search of help comes to an agency, the caseworker is faced with an inescapable time limit set by nature. If, as too often happens, the girl has avoided facing her situation until the last possible moment, the limit may be close indeed. The caseworker's immediate responsibility is to reassure the girl that practical arrangements are possible and will be made at once. But the unwed prospective mothers are in need of a great deal more than provision for prenatal and postnatal care. They are almost certainly in need of skillful casework help if they are ever to find direction in their lives.

There is also another demand on the caseworker, whose responsibility is twofold. Not only must he help the girl if the girl can accept help. He must also take every measure to assure a good life for the baby. It is important to remember that these two responsibilities are never at cross purposes, as inexperienced caseworkers sometimes fear they may be. If it is good for the unwed mother to keep her baby, then it is good for the baby to stay with the mother. The baby needs above all things assurance of love and security, and if the mother can provide them, then it is good for them to be together. If she cannot give them, either because of her social situation or because of her personality limitations, then it is bad for her to try— equally bad for mother and for child, no matter what she says she wants. The caseworker must look behind and beyond her words; he must have far more than a superficial understanding of the mother's personality, motivations, and reality situation before he can know what would be good.

In fact, before anything beyond the immediate practical plans for physical care can be provided, the caseworker must know a great deal about the girl whom he is to help. Is the girl psychotic? Is she neurotic? Is she a psychopathic personality, unable to think in terms of consequences or to show concern for anyone beyond herself? Is she a confused and insecure adolescent who was unable to find any better way than sexual promiscuity to win social acceptance? Is she, perhaps, one of a group of modern experimenters who, stirred by erotic music, movies, and stories, and offered all too easy access to privacy and freedom from chaperonage, has decided to find out what sexual experience feels like, with little thought to consequences? Or was she truly fond of the man who is the father of her child? If so, what happened to the relationship? Or was she seduced by a man more experienced than herself, perhaps even by her father? Is she perhaps from a social setting in which illegitimate pregnancy is not frowned upon, where out-of-wedlock babies are accepted and loved without criticism or comment?

Each situation would call for a different type of casework, different planning. Would the baby have a better life in an adoptive home and would the mother be better off if she were to pick up her life again without the baby, go back to school or to a job, start over? Or are the young mother's personality and background such that the baby would have as good a life with her as he might if she were married? If the community accepts illegitimacy too easily, we might wish to institute a program of social reform, but we cannot start with this baby nor with this mother.

Not, of course, that the caseworker should do a complete diagnostic study immediately when a girl first comes to the agency for help. After all, if one sees a person struggling in a whirlpool, one tries to haul him out promptly without stopping to inquire how he happened to fall in. But as the caseworker talks to the girl he will learn a great deal from what she says and from what she carefully refrains from saying. From the girl's tone and manner, the caseworker can begin to understand her attitude toward the agency, toward her own situation, toward the father of the child who is on the way, and toward the child himself. With this understanding in mind, the worker can begin to talk to the girl in terms of definite, concrete plans—immediate plans for medical care for herself and, tentatively, long-range plans for her own future and that of the baby.

Sometimes the unwed mother-to-be is an adolescent who lacks security within herself. Such a girl may permit sexual relationship with boys in a blind groping after popularity and acceptance by her peers. Or she may seek it from older men in order to find the security her own family has not provided. What such a girl needs almost as much as she needs immediate help in planning for prenatal care and delivery is emotional support from an older woman, a mother person. Perhaps the caseworker can interpret this need to the girl's parents, who may have been well meaning but unaware of their daughter's needs. However, if the parents are themselves too immature to give what is required, then it is the caseworker himself (or, more likely in this situation, the *caseworker herself*) who must provide the supportive relationship which will strengthen the girl until she can take a step or two beyond the dependency of childhood.

Probably a girl of this type will be too immature to accept the responsibilities of motherhood, and almost certainly it would be inadvisable to encourage her to keep the baby with her. Probably what is needed is emotional support throughout her pregnancy and, later, help in readjusting in school, or, if she is over school age and her intellectual abilities do not warrant further education, then help to return to her home community to start life all over again. The baby can be placed for adoption through any of the recognized adoption agencies. Many public welfare agencies act in this capacity, and there are a number of private adoption agencies.

Recently there has been considerable concern over what is termed the "new era in our attitude toward sex." Dr. Goodrich C. Schauffler, an obstetrician, says:

Children today are subjected to sex in its rawest forms before they have the faintest concept of its total meaning in life. . . . As a nation we are preoccupied—almost obsessed—with the superficial aspects of sex; you might almost say with sex as a form of amusement. It is an almost hysterical bandying about of sex symbols. . . . Consider the present overemphasis of the breast, the stressing of erotic qualities in perfume. We find this unrealistic sex in movies, in magazine illustrations, in advertisements; it is splashed on the covers of paper-backed books and through the comic magazines. . . . And so we find intelligent girls assenting to sex without love, without even considering marriage or the possibility that a baby may result.[1]

In another part of the article, Dr. Schauffler quotes a conversation with a college girl who said that "nine out of ten aren't innocent any more by their senior year."

"What about love?" asked Dr. Schauffler.
"Oh, I don't think that's essential. Most of the kids would be embarrassed to talk much about love. They are more interested in learning about life."
"Do they look forward to marrying the man they are involved with?"
"I don't think that enters in."
"What about babies?"
"Perish the thought!" [2]

Intelligent girls like the one quoted here may become pregnant out of wedlock because they are victims of too much stimulation, and too little control from their homes or their social environment. They are not emotionally disturbed and they are not neurotic. They want the thrill and the experience about which they have been hearing so much, but they have been given no concept of the meaning which the sex act can have as part of a lifelong relationship with its deeper implications of family solidarity. They go after sex experiences in about the same spirit that a two-year-old goes after the thrill of jumping off the back of the sofa, quite ignorant of the bump that follows.

For such girls pregnancy, if it comes, is punishment enough. Faced with the consequences of their impulsive behavior, they need help in their immediate planning. Later they will need help to face their home environment again, and to plan for the baby, probably through adoption. But most of all they need an intelligent interpretation of what sex can mean as part of the whole life experience. These girls will be all right if they are not too seriously damaged by what has

[1] Goodrich C. Schauffler, M.D., "Today It Could Be Your Daughter," *Ladies Home Journal,* January, 1958, p. 43. This article discusses the several motivations for out-of-wedlock pregnancy, with an especial emphasis on just this type, seen in daughters of respected, well-to-do families.
[2] *Ibid.,* p. 43.

happened. They have learned, and they will not make the same mistake again.

However, there is another type of unwed mother who is far more difficult to help. This is the seriously disoriented girl who may have a series of children by as many men. In such situations somebody must plan for the babies, since this type of mother commonly shows much less concern than a mother cat would show. She may leave her infant in the hospital after delivery, or she may leave him with a relative or a friend or in a boarding home, and then drift away without making any arrangements for his support.

Some girls of this type are unquestionably mentally retarded and should be institutionalized for their own protection. But some of them appear, in situations other than those involving sex, to have normal or nearly normal intelligence, which, however, is for the most part inaccessible for use because of emotional blocking. Unhappily, by the time these women are physically adult enough to conceive, they are usually beyond the reach of corrective casework, especially as they almost never show the slightest dissatisfaction with their way of life. Their conscience is weak or, indeed, altogether lacking. They are psychopathic personalities such as were described in Chapter VI. They have no mature acceptance of responsibility for what happens to other people (including the children they bear) and they have insufficient imagination to possess any awareness of the feelings of other people or of the child who must grow up without both his parents. They have the sex urges of a grown woman, the emotional reactions of a child. About all a caseworker can do in such circumstances is to arrange for the immediately needed prenatal and postnatal care and then try to keep track of the young mother long enough to get her signature on the surrender which will legally release her baby for adoption so that he may belong to a family of his own.

There are still other girls for whom illegitimate pregnancy is an acting out of conflicts left over from early relationships with parents. To understand and to work successfully with them, the caseworker must be aware of some of the things that happen to small human beings between the ages of two, say, and ten or thereabouts; for, strange though it may seem, it is what happens in those early years that often influences attitudes in adolescence and early adulthood. We must go back to the family relationships that affect a child during the early years of what, in psychiatric language, is called the "Oedipal period." This is the time when a child normally becomes interested in, and affectionate toward, the parent of the opposite sex. The term "Oedipal" comes from the Greek play *Oedipus Rex*, the story of a man who, having been separated in infancy from his parents, returns as an adult and, without recognizing them, kills his father and marries his mother.

The first object of a small child's outgoing affection is usually the parent who has responded most to infant needs, probably the mother. Later, his physical development and his growing curiosity prompt a natural interest in his own genitals and in those individuals whose genitals are constructed differently from his. At about this same time the child, who has begun to walk and get about by himself, is discovering that he is no longer completely dependent on mother to supply all his needs. He can ask for what he wants in a phrase more articulate than a cry. He can even go after it without asking. Moreover, he can refuse what he does not want. All children at this time find considerable pleasure in being bossy and domineering, and this shows up in his attitude toward the parent of the same sex as himself. His fascination with the parent of the opposite sex usually makes him jealous and resentful of the parent of the same sex. This is the time when little boys thump their fathers and kill them in fantasy, promising that when they are big they will get their mothers all sorts of wonderful gifts which the mean old father is withholding. It is the time when little girls sulk at their mothers and announce that when they grow up they are going to marry their fathers and live happily ever after.

This is a normal phase in human development, and it all works itself out in time if the parent of the same sex can take the temporary rejection without hurt or resentment, and if the parent of the opposite sex does not let the childish wooing turn his head and tempt him to use the flattering love to feed his own emotional hunger. A normal child in a normal family group where the emotional climate is healthy will grow out of his Oedipal attachments and begin to identify with the parent of the same sex. The little boy becomes very masculine, imitates his father, and avoids "sissy" demonstrations of affection. The girl becomes quite the little lady, wants to learn the feminine arts, and longs to be just like her mother.

It is, however, a ticklish time in which any one of a number of things can go wrong, tipping the balance against normal emotional maturation. If the relationship between the parents themselves is strained, the child, in identifying with the parent of the same sex, may imitate this attitude of antagonism and carry it over into adult life, growing up to be domineering and scornful toward all members of the opposite sex. Or possibly the child will develop into an adult who, through avoidance of any emotional relationship with members of the opposite sex, becomes homosexual. Or the child may grow into an adult who marries but fails to adjust to a normal, hetero-sexual life. Then the children of that marriage face the same dangers during their Oedipal periods—and so on, an endless chain.

Any failure to receive love from the parent of the same sex blocks the child from a normal development of identification with his own sex. If a son has had a poor relationship with a rough or rejecting father, he may regress into the safety of his earlier dependent love for his mother. The result is a mama's boy who in later life looks to his wife to fill a mother's place for him. A girl who does not learn to identify with her own sex will not be able as an adult to accept the woman's role in the home. Her identification will be with the mascu-line. She may marry but avoid motherhood; she may remain single and be a career woman; she may be homosexual, either overtly or subconsciously.

If a mother is herself immature and unfulfilled, she may uncon-sciously use a male child's demonstrative affection to fill her own emotional needs, responding to her small boy's eager love with an answering seductiveness which encourages him to remain in the emotionally rewarding Oedipal phase instead of moving into iden-tification with his own sex. This is the silver cord, the "smother love" so bitterly denounced in song and story but still so tragically preva-lent. Similarly, a father, especially if his marriage is not a happy one, may wreck havoc on his daughter's life.

The results of any of these various types of early damage may be obvious during a child's adolescence or in the years following. A caseworker whose client is an illegitimately pregnant girl must be alert to the possibility that something was amiss during the Oedipal period in the girl's life. Not, of course, that any caseworker would ever under any circumstances use this phrase in talking to the girl. The girl's conscious attention is, and should be, centered on the present and the immediate problems of her current situation, but the watchful caseworker will find clues in the girl's attitude that will indicate clearly what happened to her years before. Aware of this, the caseworker can make plans based on the girl's personality, unconscious and unexpressed though it is.

One constantly recurring situation is that of the illegitimately pregnant girl who comes from a home dominated by one possessive parent. Perhaps the parents are separated, perhaps they have remained together, but the effect on the girl is the same if she has come almost exclusively under the emotional domination of one parent. If the parents have remained together, one of them may be quite obviously weak or irresponsible. Or the situation may not be obvious at all. The girl's parents may present a surface picture of a happy home life, prompting neighbors to wonder how an ungrateful girl from such a home would ever "go wrong." This appearance of a smooth marital partnership can easily occur since a neurotically dominating person usually selects a submissive marriage mate. In such a case there is no throwing of crockery, no shouting, no friction to be seen from the outside. However, such a marriage cannot be a partnership; it is a rivalry, with the submissive member invariably the loser and the daughter the personal possession of the dominant one.

If the husband is the dominant one, he may be a man of no warmth who discourages all overtures of affection from his daughters, who must go into and out of the early Oedipal phase without any emotional satisfaction and without the normal response from the father. In such a family constellation the wife often submits to this mastery, even encourages it with masochistic pleasure. The daughter almost always resents it, but fearing her father too much to resent openly, she transfers her resentment to any unfortunate boy who pays attention to her. If this relationship results in an out-of-wedlock pregnancy, as it often does, the girl's attitude toward the boy is one of hatred and punishment. She usually wants to use the baby as a club over the head of her lover. Not only does she use all possible legal pressure to demand support, but she often utilizes the baby as a means to embarrass the man, breaking up his home if he is already married, or even hounding him out of his place of employment.

This is an exceedingly difficult situation for a caseworker to handle. Because of the highly unsatisfactory relationship which the girl has had with her own father, she finds it almost impossible to believe in a healthy relationship with any man. Emotionally, this girl is not a woman but is still a small, angry child kicking furiously against too rigid discipline or the frustration of being unloved. She cannot accept any man as a partner because she unconsciously identifies all men with her father, whom she hates and fears. Such a girl often expresses affection and pity for her mother but seldom respect. "She's more like a sister to me," she will say. She cannot relate to a female caseworker in any fashion that would make help possible because she identifies all women with her weak and helpless mother. She has never learned to expect kindness and strength in the same individual. The caseworker's job here is to get the baby in a position where he cannot be used as a tool in the hands of a neurotic girl, but can grow up free and loved, an individual in his own right. This goal is often far from easy to accomplish, since a neurotic girl is not going to relinquish readily the visible proof of her power to punish. Sometimes a man caseworker is more effective with this type of girl than a woman caseworker. If he is strong and kind and very, very patient, he may in time be accepted by her as a father figure. Then, if he is skillful, he may be able to help her develop from a resentful small child to a mature woman able to enter into a normal marriage partnership. Sometimes, however, this type of girl is beyond saving, and the only recourse is to bring court action against her, demanding support for the child so that he becomes, not an easy tool to her hand but a heavy responsibility she is willing to release. This strategy at least rescues the baby.

Sometimes the unmarried mothers come from homes where the father was the dominant figure but not a domineering one. He may have been overaffectionate, asking for an unhealthy degree of demonstrative return from his daughter, tempting her to remain in the Oedipal phase for the gratification it provides instead of moving on to an identification with her own sex. These fathers are often unhappy in their own marital relationships, perhaps openly critical of their wives. Some daughters of such fathers may marry, but they are not likely to be successful wives either because they are still emotionally dependent on their fathers, or because they cannot accept the feminine role of wife and mother. If these girls become illegitimately pregnant, they commonly show little interest in the father of the baby, having in a completely subconscious fantasy placed their own father in that role. They often want to take the baby back to their father's home and to live there in a dislocated and fantastic husband-wife-child relationship that is unconscious on the part of everyone—and unhealthy. These girls are not easy to work with, for they are completely unaware of their own motivation, and would be damaged, not helped, by any interpretation. A man caseworker cannot often help, since this girl is already getting emotional satisfaction from her father, even though on such an infantile level. Once in a while she can be reached through the father if his social position is seriously threatened by the presence of an out-of-wedlock grandchild. Psychiatric analysis might help if the girl will accept it.

If the mother is the dominant parent, the daughter's problem as well as her reaction will be different. Usually such a girl, if she becomes pregnant, will arrive at the agency accompanied by her mother. Even if she comes alone, she is likely to say, "I'll do whatever mother says," or, "I want the baby to be adopted. My mother says that would be best." The daughter of this sort of mother has usually lived all her life at home, and expects to go back home after delivery, with or without the baby—whichever mother advises. Sometimes these girls are spunky enough to resent the mother and defy her wishes, but the effect is the same, since in neither case do the girls think for themselves; they only try to find out what mother wants, and then do it, or else do the opposite. Either way, it is what mother says that determines the direction of events.

These mother-dominated girls are frequently found in homes where the father is dead or has deserted and the mother has been obliged to support her children. It is not always the authoritative manner which makes for domination; it can be accomplished just as well, or even better, by self-sacrifice. The daughter who has been held in emotional bondage by such a mother may have a strong resentment and an even stronger feeling of guilt because of that resentment. This is revealed frequently in such speeches as, "I don't know how I could have done this to my mother"; or, "I'll do anything to make up to mother for what I've done to her."

It must not be forgotten for a moment that the motives that prompt these girls are wholly unconscious. They say, and they believe that they mean it, that they love their babies. But their behavior proves they are not thinking of the child as an individual who will grow older, go to school, become an adult; they are thinking of him as a tool to prove something to mother. These girls, like the father-dominated daughters, are still children held prisoner in their emotional dependence on a parent. They have not been able to develop far enough to identify in any mature fashion with their own sex. There is, however, one hopeful element here. If this type of unmarried mother is not too infantile or too much disturbed, she may be able to accept and use casework help. If such a girl can transfer her dependence from her own mother to the caseworker, there is a good chance that she can be led out of emotional infancy into a more mature insight and some degree of independence through this relationship.

Clearly, it is important that a caseworker should be able to recognize which type of girl he is dealing with. This does not mean that the caseworker should ask a series of probing questions at the initial interview. Usually, the unmarried pregnant girl has come to the agency miserably unhappy, confused (so far as her conscious mind is aware), not knowing where she is to go for medical help or for the privacy she needs. She may fear her father's anger, or she may think she is afraid of her mother's reproaches. The caseworker, facing a time limit, must make realistic plans promptly and ask diagnostic questions later. If the caseworker is friendly, nonjudgmental, practical, the girl's confidence may strengthen bit by bit until in time she may accept the caseworker as the strong, unpossessive parent she never had. The caseworker may then be able to lead the girl toward emotional independence and maturity. If this does not happen, there is nothing much the caseworker can do except meet the external needs and be ready to accept the baby for adoption if the moment comes when the unwed mother can give up this unfortunate tool for punishment.

CHAPTER XVI

Adoption

THIS CHAPTER will not be an exposition on how to arrange for some nice couple to adopt a baby. It will not be an explanation of how to get some nice baby adopted. It will, frankly, be an argument against a worker's doing anything whatever about adoption without the advice and coöperation of an authorized adoption agency. It is written in the hope of persuading the reader that neither doctor nor pastor nor lawyer nor the kindly neighbor next door should undertake to place any child for adoption unless an agency acts as an intermediary. The agency must turn to doctor, pastor, lawyer, and neighbor for help, but, conversely, so should these latter depend on the agency to do what they cannot do.

In a private, or nonagency, adoption, the biological mother surrenders the child directly to the adoptive parents at the time when the petition for adoption is brought before the court by the lawyer who represents the adoptive couple. The court cannot entertain the petition until the child has been in the adoptive home for a certain period of time, which varies from one state to another. At any time during this period of waiting, which ranges from three months to a year, the natural mother has the full legal right to reclaim her child. Mothers sometimes take this step, and it always causes bitter disappointment to the adoptive parents, who have learned to love their new baby very much.

Even after the legalization of such an adoption, the own mother can, and sometimes does, make an emotional claim on the child. She knows the name of the adoptive parents and probably where they live. She can upset them by calling at their home to pour out her grief and regret for what she has done. Or years later she may confuse the child tragically by demanding an emotional response from him for a "mother" he has never heard of. If the biological mother goes so far as to ask that the adoption be abrogated by court action, she can secure a lawyer to take such a petition before a judge. The adoptive family must then fight the action in court, quite probably plagued by widespread publicity which can only harm the child no matter what the outcome of the court action.

By no means all private adoptions have unfortunate consequences. If a man adopts his wife's child by a previous marriage, there is not likely to be any difficulty. If a couple should take the child of a relative who cannot care for him, the arrangements have doubtless been thoroughly discussed in advance. We are thinking rather of the adoption in which a couple who very much want a child, and cannot have their own, take into their home the child of an unmarried mother. Often, of course, the adoption is a happy one, but everybody, unwed mother, adoptive parents, and baby, runs a risk.

Look first at the unwed mother. The last chapter has shown how complicated and confused the emotions of an illegitimately pregnant girl may be. During the pregnancy she is almost certain to be miserably unhappy and frightened of the future. Right up to the time of delivery she may feel that all she wants is to avoid the consequences that face her. Other reactions may come later, and usually do. If she tells someone during her pregnancy that she never wants to see the baby, or if while she is still half in shock following delivery she asks the doctor to relieve her of all future responsibility for the baby, that will not mean she may not change her mind a month later. The only way to help the unmarried mother is to give her time to think things through—not so much time, of course, that for years the baby is nobody's child, but a month or two while she recovers her strength, her health, her sense of proportion. Maybe she can make realistic plans to keep her baby and care for him herself, but if she surrenders him for adoption it should be because she realizes that to do so is the best way, perhaps the only way, to provide a good life for him. It is rarely that an unmarried girl has the emotional maturity or the stability to reach a definite conclusion about her own life or her baby's without time and without casework help. It is not fair to the girl to encourage her to commit herself before she is ready. Even if she does not later create confusion and unhappiness by reclaiming her baby before the adoption is made final in court, she may be left with a burden of unresolved guilt and confused emotions that will hamper her all her life. She deserves a chance to be helped to see herself and her child clearly and realistically.

Commonly in private adoptions the baby is placed in the adoptive home directly from the hospital a few days after birth, and it is in these circumstances that the adoptive parents incur a risk. They may know little if anything of the baby's background, and they have no opportunity to assess his potential for development. They may all unknowingly be taking into their hearts and their home a child with serious inherited defects. Retrolental fibroplasia, a type of blindness, cannot be diagnosed before a child is five or six weeks old. Familial type of mental retardation might be suspected from a known background, but cannot be certainly known at birth. Some adoptive parents can give such unfortunate children everything they need of love, security, and special care. But some cannot, and it can mean only tragedy if parents who have not the necessary financial means, or the greatheartedness, to care for such a child find that they have adopted an atypical child with special needs. If they cannot care for him, or cannot love him as they hoped, they will be beset by doubts of themselves, by conflict, by guilt.

The baby takes a chance, too. In a private adoption no effort is made to secure factual information about the adoptive home and family, or about the psychological and emotional factors present. One of the facts of life which every caseworker learns is that people do not always mean what they say. They do not even mean what they think they mean. A couple who hope to adopt a baby will usually say that they love babies and yearn for one in their home. Quite possibly that is so, but it may not be the whole truth. The marriage may be on the point of breaking up, and the wife may trust that a child will hold the home together. But that is too much responsibility to put on a baby. Almost certainly the marriage will crack anyway if it was headed toward dissolution, and then the child will be left in a broken home or, at best, in a loveless home where he must hear constant argument and recrimination. Or perhaps the adoptive couple may be emotionally unstable, one of the pair may want the child in order to fill a neurotic need, such as a need for power, or a need to smother some small creature with a too possessive love. The financial circumstances may be bad, or the moral environment unsuitable for a child. The baby has no choice, and in a private adoption no one examines the situation so as to make a wise choice for him.

The argument is sometimes put forward that babies may be born to own parents who are unstable, neurotic, or immoral. This is all too true, but it does not follow that we are justified in deliberately permitting a child to be placed in such a home when a better one can be chosen for him. Any baby takes enough chances just being born without facing the addition of avoidable hazards.

Agency adoptions are not always perfect either, but some of the risks are definitely avoided and others are reduced. If an unmarried pregnant girl applies to an agency for help she gets the financial and medical assistance she needs for prenatal and postnatal care and delivery. She also gets whatever casework help she needs and can accept, the counseling that carries her through the period of turmoil, confusion, and contradictory emotions until she can think clearly and decide realistically whether she can take care of her baby or whether it would be better both for herself and for him to surrender him for adoption. If she decides in favor of surrender, she signs the paper that gives the agency the right to place the baby for adoption. From that moment the agency acts for the protection of the baby and for the security of any adoption which is subsequently planned.

Meanwhile, the baby has usually been taken from the hospital to a foster home where he remains until the biological mother has fully decided what she wants to do. During the period of working with the mother, the same agency arranges for the baby to have all necessary physical and medical care, and a psychological evaluation as soon as such an evaluation has any meaning. By the time the own mother decides on surrender, if she does, a great deal is known about the infant's heredity, his family background, his health problems, if any, and his psychological potential. The adoptive parents can be selected with all these factors in mind.

Adoption agencies make an effort to get acquainted with couples who ask to adopt a child, learning as much as they can about the financial, moral, and emotional factors. They try to find the right couple to meet a particular child's needs, looking less for riches and a fine home than for warmth, stability, and willingness to accept the baby as an individual who will presently be not a cuddly infant, but a growing child, then an adolescent, then a young adult.

Often the same agency which works with the biological parent and with the baby is working simultaneously with the adoptive couple, but sometimes it is another agency which studies the couple who hope to adopt. If that is the case there will be detailed discussion between the two agencies and an exchange of information before a decision is reached to offer any particular infant to prospective parents.

The prospective parents are given all the information about the child's background and health history which could possibly affect his development. If the background is questionable, the parents need not take this child but can wait for another. If they are the kind of people who can love their adopted child no matter what his background, no matter what his limitations, they will take him, with the knowledge of what they may have to face in the future. They do not meet the biological mother, whose anonymity is preserved, nor does the natural mother ever meet the adoptive parents. She has already surrendered her child to an agency which she must have learned to trust to do the best for her child.

When a child is placed by an agency, that agency helps the new family become a unit. Before legal finalization, during the three months, or six, or a year that the state requires as a trial period, the agency stands by, not to "check up" on the adoptive parents, but to help and protect both them and the child. There is not much probability that a biological mother who has worked over a certain length of time with an agency should change her mind. She has been given a chance to think, and an opportunity to talk things through. But if she should reconsider her decision after her child has been placed in an adoptive home, she cannot disrupt that home, for she does not know its name or its location. She must apply to the agency to whom the surrender was made, and the agency will use all its experience, all its casework skill, to decide what is best for the mother, the child, and the adoptive parents. If the own mother does persist in asking for a court abrogation of the adoption, it is the agency which must meet that petition in court, thus providing protection for the adoptive parents.

There are two arguments sometimes brought forward against agency adoptions—two, that is, in addition to the completely specious and untenable one already mentioned to the effect that since a biological birth carries hazards, no one should bother to make adoptions any safer. One argument, the validity of which the agencies cannot deny, is that when a couple works through an agency, they face a probable delay of months, whereas private adoptions may be practically instantaneous, with no long-drawn-out investigation. A young wife may learn from her doctor that there is no possibility that she and her husband can ever have a child of their own blood, either because of her physical disability or because of her husband's infertility, and almost in the next moment she may learn from this same doctor of an out-of-wedlock infant born that day in the hospital and available for placement. It may be as fast as that, with no questions asked on either side. The doctor may know his patient as a cultured woman from a respectable family, but he has given himself no time to find out how she is resolving her feelings about her inability to have a child of her own. The adoptive baby this couple takes so hastily may be forever a symbol to them of their infertility, or he may become the helpless object through which the wife tries to work out her frustrated maternal instinct, never permitting him to mature into independence and to develop his own personality. Or the baby himself may be unable to grow into the kind of child the adoptive family visualize as their child. The delay in placement and the prolonged investigation made by agencies are deliberate measures to insure the future happiness of both child and parents. And that objective should be worth the wait.

Another argument offered against agency adoptions is that when an adoptive couple work through an agency they must reveal to the caseworker a great many details which may be embarrassing and painful to bring into the open. This cannot be denied. An adoptive couple must face with the caseworker things to which they may have been closing their eyes in fear—the true nature of their relationship to one another; their feeling about the sexual aspect of their marriage; their attitude toward their own parents; their experience, if any, with babies or small children; how much they realize of the change which the advent of a baby will create in their social and domestic life; their deepest reactions to their own childlessness; their willingness to be frank with the child about his status as adopted; their feelings about a poor background or a possible handicap in a child. Any of these may be factors which the agency feels will determine how successful they can be as parents to a small, out-of-wedlock, unwanted baby. And the couple must face the possibility that after all the painful self-revelation, they may not be accepted by the agency as adoptive parents.

The answer to all this is that the adoptive agency is searching for the best possible parents for the child that has been surrendered for placement. The caseworker must know, must be *sure*, for the sake of the baby. Moreover, in the course of the study, the adoptive parents themselves may grow in stature, learn to know themselves and their own motives as they never have before. The couple who can become the best adoptive parents enter into the study, not perhaps with confidence, but with a clear awareness that they will take the bitter along with the sweet for the sake of the baby that may be placed in their home and perhaps for the sake of the self-knowledge they win.

CHAPTER XVII

The aged

MEDICAL SKILLS have added years to human life but have done little to make those extra years pleasant or profitable. Today a man may live to be ninety-five who a generation ago might have died in middle life of pneumonia or a cardiac complication or anemia or diabetes or any one of a number of ailments that now can be cured or controlled. But nothing so far has been found to forestall the slackening of the muscles, the stiffening of the joints, the slowing of the vital processes, the dulling of the senses. There must come one sad day when a man is forced to face the grim fact that old age is upon him, and then he needs help as he has never needed it before. The old, like the young, have emotional needs that must be met if life is to be happy and complete. They need a sense of security, a feeling of being wanted and loved, a conviction that they are accomplishing something, and the assurance of acceptance in a group.

Does the list of emotional needs sound familiar? It should, for these are the needs of the infant, the child, the adolescent, the adult. The difference is that each day's development in the life of a child brings him closer to maturity when he can make an effort in his own behalf to find his satisfactions. The difference is that a normal, healthy adult can control his environment and direct his behavior toward the satisfaction of his needs. But time is carrying the aged person farther from the ability to help himself. Every day, strength, skills, abilities, are slipping away from him. He needs help.

Federal Social Security, private retirement plans, grants from Old Age Assistance, are all helping to forestall the loss of financial security. There is no reason today in this country why an old person should not be adequately if not elegantly cared for so far as food and lodging are concerned. Clinics, hospital insurance, Public Assistance, make medical care available to the aged whether or not they have funds of their own.

But the other basic needs of the aged are not so adequately met. A normal adult can satisfy his yearning for affection through marital and family relationships, but the aged person has often outlived his marriage mate and worn out his welcome in the family group. The healthy adult satisfies his need for achievement through his job, or through his (or her) contribution to a smoothly running home life. But the old person may have been forcibly retired from his employment, or, if not, he must certainly face the realization that he is no longer able to accomplish what he could ten years earlier. Thrown into competition with younger, faster, more skillful workers, or even in comparison with his own previous accomplishments, the old person loses all feeling of satisfactory achievement. He may grow depressed by a sense of his own uselessness, of being a burden, or he may project his feeling of failure and bitterly blame his family or his erstwhile employer for lack of appreciation of his years of experience and service. Whichever reaction accords with his temperament, he is not happy.

The whole situation is made more grievous for the old person by the simultaneous loss of a feeling of acceptance in a group. The normal adult satisfies that need through contacts with fellow workers, through clubs or social life, through neighborhood activities. But the old person has no job, he cannot keep up with the changing interests and chatter of young people, and he is probably unable to travel far enough to visit his surviving contemporaries.

If the old person is still living with relatives there may well be added problems for him and for the family with whom he lives. As an aging person's strength fails, he may lose his concern for personal tidiness. With weakening sphincter muscles, he may become incontinent. He may avoid the "nuisance" of bathing, cling to familiar soiled clothing, spill his food as he eats. Not too secure of his place in the group, he is easily offended if these matters are mentioned. Unable because of increasing physical limitations to grasp new ideas or keep abreast of current events, he talks end-lessly of the past, telling and retelling tales of his own early years in a pathetic effort to bolster his sense of achievement, and he is hurt if he is interrupted. With the slowing of circulation, the brain is deprived of an adequate blood supply, so that thinking is slower, memory is impaired, judgment is poor. The oldster resents being supervised, but often he cannot safely be left alone. All too fre-quently the active, younger members of the family are irked by the burden and show it.

Here, then, is the situation into which the geriatric caseworker moves. First, he should make quite certain that the old person actually does have the financial aid to which he is entitled by the government's assumption of responsibility. This should be sufficient to meet minimal needs for board and lodging and medical care. Whatever the sources of the income, whether help from relatives, or a grant from Old Age Assistance, it is to be hoped that it is given graciously, not grudgingly. The limited funds available to the aged person may force a reduction in his standard of living—less money for tobacco, fewer dollars to contribute to his church, less to offer his son-in-law in payment for board. If the help comes in the form of a grant from public assistance, it is the responsibility of the case-worker to interpret the budget, and sometimes it is almost impossi-ble to do so in a way that the old person can accept. It is hard not to be independent after years of taking care of oneself. It is hard not to be able to buy gifts for the grandchildren, or make donations to the Community Chest. But the caseworker must try to interpret agency limitations patiently and courteously, so that even if the oldster does not like the amount of his grant he is nevertheless convinced that the worker cares what is happening to him, and this is the best that can be done.

Financial help is available, and it can be provided sympatheti-cally. It may be rather more difficult for the worker to arrange for the satisfaction of the need for affection. Love cannot be turned on like a stream from a faucet, and there is no reasonable facsimile. The failing of the aged person's physical and mental faculties may make him less lovable, and all too often will react on his disposition, thus adding to the problem. Although most people feel sympathetic

toward physical frailty, it is more difficult to be tolerant of queru-
lousness and tantrums. But the loss of functioning brain cells through
atrophy or through arteriosclerosis may cause personality changes,
depression, hallucinations, delusions of persecution. Dr. Fish says:

For better or worse society remains far more tolerant of physical than
of psychic affliction. A family may thus be quite tolerant of physical
dependency, almost as tolerant of forgetfulness (which they recognize as
due to brain impairment) but openly critical and punitive toward emotional outbursts.[1]

If an old person's presence in the family group is creating friction,
perhaps the worker can provide a clear and factual explanation to
the impatient family of just what is happening to their relative's
bones, muscles, organs, circulation, and nervous system. If there
has ever been real love felt for the oldster such an interpretation
may possibly tip the balance in favor of love as against exasperation. But to succeed in this effort the worker must not only know
something of the physiology of age; he must also be able to see
the problem of the family, and must avoid any hint of criticism
that might stir guilt or resentment on the part of the younger members of the group. If his efforts fail and the family cannot accept
the oldster's limitations, then all the worker can do is provide as
best he can the supportive relationship himself. Either that, or arrange for the old fellow to move to a more sympathetic environment.

Sometimes, in fact, everyone, including the aged person himself,
is happier if the oldster does not try to live with his family but
moves to an institution where he can find companionship with
others of his generation. In *Old Man Minick*, a play by George
Kaufman and Edna Ferber, the old man's son and daughter-in-law
offer him a home. They do their best, but they find themselves
growing tense and edgy because of their hampered social life and
the intrusion on their privacy. Old Man Minick suddenly solves
the problem by electing to go to an institution for the aged where
his habits are not unlike those of the other old men and his opinions are greatly respected by his contemporaries. By the move he

[1] Mayer Fish, M.D., "Organic Psychiatric Disorders of the Aged: How
They Affect Family Relationships," *Social Casework,* XXXIX (1958), 506.

finds acceptance in a group, a feeling of status, and a release from the suspicion that he might be a nuisance.

The caseworker will find, however, that not all old people are by temperament fitted to group living. Sometimes an old codger has decided that he will give up group acceptance in favor of the security of the familiar. He wants nothing so much as to be let alone to live by himself in some shanty of his own choosing, willing to forego physical comforts in return for independence and the right to live his own life in his own obstinate way, unmolested by what any bright young person thinks is good for him. This situation often tests the worker's skill. The aged person, like any client, has the right of choice. It is what he wants, not what the worker thinks he should want, that is important. But there remains a reality factor. The old fellow may think he is more capable than he actually is, and then it takes a nice balancing of values on the part of the worker to decide what to do. The old person has the right to select solitude rather than gregariousness; he can even live in dirt rather than in cleanliness if he likes. But he should not be permitted to freeze to death in the winter because he has overestimated his ability to keep a supply of wood on hand. He should not be allowed to lie helpless for days because he has forgotten that old bones are brittle. Nor should his way of life be permitted to create a fire hazard in the community.

Each situation must be decided as it comes up. There are no general rules that apply to all—except this one: make the old person feel certain that you are concerned for him, that you want what is right for him. Sometimes a visit to the home for the aged, to see what the place is really like, will make it easier for the oldster to relinquish his dangerous solitude.

Some communities do a great deal for their aged population. Industries have been organized to provide employment to men and women who are beyond the usual retirement age. Job requirements are tempered to the pace and the abilities of old people, and it has been found that their experience, their loyalty, their conscientiousness, are economic assets. Even where no industry has been set up specifically for the aged, the caseworker can sometimes locate job openings if he uses ingenuity and a little judicious publicity. Even those for whom salaried jobs are out of the question may be given some sense of accomplishment by means of hobbies. Knitting, crocheting, making earrings from buttons, devising artificial buttonhole bouquets—these are only a few of the possibilities. Boredom is one of the curses of old age. Sometimes clubs or church organizations can be interested in helping old people feel wanted. If a person is confined to one room, his eyesight too poor to permit reading or watching television, with fingers too arthritic to undertake any kind of handiwork, perhaps with hearing too dull to understand the radio, then the hours can drag indeed, and an afternoon caller or an auto ride can lighten a dreary day.

Whatever it is that the caseworker finds to help the aged individual face the inescapable circumstances of his life, he must keep in mind the cardinal rules of casework. It is what the client wants and how the client feels that are important, not what the worker thinks he ought to want. The client is an individual, not a type, not a Case, not a category of Old Age Assistance. He is himself, unique, and different from all other individuals. The caseworker would do well to remember, too, that if he lives long enough, he too will some day be an old person, in need of the same consideration, tact, patience, and understanding that he is giving now.

CHAPTER XVIII

Client-worker relationship

THE RELATIONSHIP between the worker and the client is of the utmost importance. It is basic. If the contact is to be of any value at all, the client must have confidence in the worker's good faith, and the worker must have respect for the client as an individual. This should be true in even the briefest of contacts—between applicant and intake worker, for example—even if the client will be referred to another worker or another agency after one interview. It should be true between doctor and patient, even if the physical examination is purely routine. It should be true between nurse and patient, between employee and personnel director, between any two people one of whom is giving, the other receiving. This feeling of confidence on one side and respect on the other is the starting point of all casework relationships. Many of them go farther and delve deeper, but this is where they must start.

It is the responsibility of the caseworker to establish this relationship. Regardless of the extent of his training, if he is the right sort for his job, he will always have respect for his client as an individual; and when he has experience and skill, he will be able through his interviewing techniques to build in the client a confidence in his good faith. The confidence may grow slowly if the client is resistant or by temperament untrustful, but until it exists casework can hardly be said to begin.

The best type of client-worker relationship is based on the worker's awareness of the client's problem and of his personality, and on the client's appreciation of the worker not as seen through a haze of transference but as the worker actually is. It is then a reality relationship built on the response of the client to the worker's words, appearance, attitude, intentions. But sometimes, no matter how skilled the worker, the relationship slides away into a realm of projected memory and fantasy. Whether or not it does this depends in part on the emotional maturity of the client and in part on the nature of the need which prompted the relationship in the first place. If the client's problem involves a need for emotional support, and if that need goes deep enough, the client may unconsciously project onto the worker attitudes he once experienced from some potent figure of his early childhood.

Annette Garrett has described the situation:

The need to ask for help recreates to some extent in anyone a dependency situation analogous to one's infancy and thus tends to reactivate the characteristic way of handling problems which was developed at that time. As a child seeks help from his parents, as a patient seeks aid from his analyst, a social work client asks for assistance from his caseworker. Even the simple request for financial assistance places one in a position of seeking favorable response from a person in power. When the help requested is more extensive than this, the feeling of dependency is proportionately greater. It is impossible for a person to place himself for long in such a dependency position without a transference to this new situation of his infantile attitudes. Part of this transference will be positive, corresponding to the love felt for the parental figure; part of it will be negative, corresponding to the fear of anyone's possessing such power over one's own destinies.[1]

Suppose we take a fairly simple example. An adolescent girl is having difficulty at home and in school. Let us say that there is constant friction between her and her parents. Because the tensions in the home are reacting unfavorably on her schoolwork, she turns for help to a guidance director, or a school nurse, or a favorite teacher, or perhaps to an agency caseworker; the selection depends probably on the school and the community organization. Since we are supposing that the girl voluntarily seeks out the person whom she asks for help we can assume that she already has faith in that person, so that the client-worker relationship has an auspicious beginning. The worker listens to the girl's troubles and

[1] Annette Garrett, "Worker-Client Relationship," *American Journal of Orthopsychiatry*, XIX, No. 2 (1949), 506; reprinted in *Ego Psychology and Dynamic Casework* (New York: Child Welfare League of America, 1957), p. 55.

does what he can in a practical way. Perhaps he rearranges the girl's school program; perhaps he introduces her to social groups acceptable both to her parents and to herself. But perhaps what is chiefly required is a supportive relationship, often the greatest need of an adolescent in the rebellious throes of working out an independence from family ties. If such a support is supplied, then what well may happen is that the girl begins to feel toward the worker as she felt when she was very small toward her father, or her doting grandparent, or perhaps an aunt who was always there to comfort her, to be on her side. The degree of emotional satisfaction which a client gets from such an unconscious transference is far beyond the realistic limits of the true worker-client relationship, and may be damaging to the client since it can tempt him to stay in an unrealistic, infantile dependence instead of moving on to self-reliance. If, in our example, circumstances make it necessary for the worker to deny the girl something she wants, that denial may reactivate the early resentment she once felt toward some early disciplinary figure in her life, and she will begin to show animosity toward the caseworker, quite as unrealistic in its basis as the earlier dependence.

Richard Sterba cites another example.[2] After a worker had established a very good positive relationship with a client, the latter asked if the worker would try to help a younger sister in difficulties. The worker agreed, but almost at once the relationship with the first client began to suffer. She arrived late for appointments, or missed them altogether, or, if she came, seemed suddenly unable to talk freely to the worker. It developed that the original client had been deeply jealous at the time of her younger sister's birth, and she was now reliving the same jealousy in her relationship with the worker that she had once felt toward her mother, who seemed to give too much attention to the baby sister—and this in spite of the fact that it was the client herself who had brought the younger sister into the picture this time. It was almost as though she had felt a need to relive the forgotten jealousy. The example shows quite clearly the unconscious nature of the transference. Only

[2] Richard Sterba, M.D., *Transference in Casework* (New York: Family Service Association of America, 1949), p. 5.

when it was interpreted and brought into the open by the worker did the client-worker relationship improve.

An experienced caseworker will watch for some sort of transference on the part of the client and will not be taken by surprise, nor will he be inclined to regard either a positive or a negative attitude as directed toward him personally. He will be ready to make use of the positive transference, which, among other advantages, will hold the client to the worker with sufficient strength to keep him from terminating the treatment prematurely, and will incline him to be hospitable to plans which the worker suggests. The worker may be able to use even negative transference, but whether he can or not, he will not be offended by the client's antagonism.

Various clues will suggest that a transference is pending: "I was very fond of my grandmother. I remember her wearing a dress just the color of the one you have on." "That's exactly the kind of thing my father always told me." Or, perhaps, "My aunt was always sticking her nose into my affairs, too." When he is aware of the imminence of transference, the worker must be prepared to control it. A prolonged positive transference may afford the client so much satisfaction in the infantile role that he will not want to move out of it toward the independence which should be the end and aim of all casework. If the worker suspects that this may be happening, he should hold the interviews closely to the external reality factors of whatever problems the client has presented rather than permit too much discussion of the emotional elements or the personality problems. His own comments, when they touch on the emotional, should be general rather than specific and personal. He may say, "People often feel dependent" rather than, "You feel dependent on me."

Since the caseworker is human himself, he will inevitably have some sort of personal reaction to each client. It is only natural that he should enjoy working with certain ones more than with others. He will like some, dislike others; find some stimulating, others boring or irritating. He will feel sympathy or impatience or admiration in response to the actual personality of the client. This is a normal reality feeling, and a caseworker readily learns that these feelings must be controlled, that they cannot be allowed to influence his work with his client. To do this is relatively easy for any conscientious worker. What is more difficult to recognize and control is the worker's unconscious response to the client's unconscious transference. This type of response on the part of the worker, known in psychiatric terminology as "countertransference," can falsify the worker's picture of a situation and seriously distort his diagnosis of both the client's personality and his problem. Then we have transference and countertransference, the blind leading the blind into a morass of emotion with no clear picture of the present reality and no practical plan to help the present situation.

Psychiatrists avoid this pitfall by undergoing analysis themselves so that they are aware of their early emotions which had been forgotten by the conscious mind until analysis pulled them out of the subconscious into the light of day. Psychoanalysis is usually neither practical nor desirable for caseworkers who do not and should not work with clients on any deep subconscious level as psychiatry does. But a caseworker can make an effort to know himself so that he can consciously allow for his own prejudices and his own characteristic reactions that stem from forgotten early experiences. One way for him to achieve this self-awareness is to study as impartially as he can his own performance as a caseworker. Has he felt in every case he has ever handled that the wife is to blame for all the marital difficulties and that the husband is to be pitied and regarded with sympathy? It is not likely that this attitude is justified in *every* case. Or does he always feel resentful of the parent when there is a parent-child conflict? The parent cannot always be in the wrong. A caseworker who consistently favors one side or the other must be especially careful to watch his unconscious reactions, and he must make a special effort to hear with complete fairness all sides of any story.

A worker's ability to understand is of first importance in any casework relationship. Perhaps not of *first* importance—before that comes the interest in people, the ability to care, the deep curiosity as to what makes humanity tick, and the strong inner need to do something to make human beings tick more smoothly. The principal advantage of casework as a profession (which usually offers all too little in status or material reward) is that it does channel to the advantage of the human race that curiosity about people and interest in them. But granting the motivating force, an understanding of the client is of most importance. Curiosity without understanding would be diffuse and purposeless. Sympathy without understanding would be soft, sentimental, and dangerous in that it might prompt the worker to do for the client what this particular client does not want, or what he might far better learn to do for himself. We have said repeatedly that without an understanding of the kind of person the client is the casework plan would be a hit-or-miss affair, and might even a little more easily be a bad miss. Only with understanding can we know what kind of help is required, what plan of help the client can use.

But there is still another purpose in understanding the inner emotional needs of the client. Even if external circumstances determine the immediate direction of the casework service, as often happens, only an understanding of the client's personality can make that plan acceptable or useful. Remember Mrs. Horton in Chapter VIII. With a crippled husband, a small child, and no financial resources she clearly needed a grant of assistance. So much was obvious even to the worker who had no understanding of Mrs. Horton's personality. But after that was supplied, the client did not use it to advantage until she was given some understanding by a more sensitive caseworker. The sensitivity to know how a client feels, the knowledge which makes it possible to guess what may have happened along life's way to prompt him to feel as he does, are necessary in any client-worker relationship. The worker may never mention his awareness—probably will not—but with the understanding comes always a subtle, perhaps unconscious, change in the worker's attitude, expressed by his face, his posture, his tone of voice. Invariably, *invariably*, the client responds to that changed attitude, with perhaps an easier acceptance of the limitations of the assistance given, with more willingness to try to help himself, with more cooperation.

With the caseworker's understanding and the client's response to that unspoken understanding comes the willingness on the part of both client and worker to make the planning a cooperative affair. Any attempt to help a person is effective only in so far as it has the active participation of the person to be helped. The worker's aim is always to make life more bearable and more productive for the client, either by changing the circumstances of his life or by changing his attitude toward those circumstances. If it is to be the latter, the worker quite obviously *must* have the client's cooperation. Threats and the "big stick" of authority will change his behavior only temporarily, if at all, and probably will not change his attitude in the least. Or if it does, the change will be for the worse, toward resentment. If the plan involves a change in the client's situation, it will be more effective if the client takes an active part in bringing about the change. Even with children, or with people so retarded that not much in the way of realistic planning can possibly be expected of them, some little bit of participation makes the client a part of the plan. Perhaps it is only that he selects the belongings that are to go with him when he is moved to another home. Maybe it is talking the whole thing over with him in language he can grasp, or persuading him to say what sort of room he would like to have amongst the rooms available. Even that small bit of participation will make him feel less that things are being done to him and more that he is doing something for himself. If he has been given no sense of sharing he can easily ruin the best laid arrangements. If his age and capacity permit really active cooperation, it should by all means be utilized. Planning may move more slowly that way, but the effects will be more lasting.

This approach is especially important in the case of children who are to be removed from their own home. If, for example, a delinquent child is to be placed in a corrective institution, the effectiveness of the institution's program will depend wholly on the attitude of the child toward his placement. Benefits come sooner if the move can be made deliberately so that acceptance on the part of the child and his psychological cooperation can at least be a possibility at the time of his admission.

Client-worker relationship, then, depends on the worker's awareness of the client's reaction to him, both the conscious, surface response and the unconscious response which is a transference to him by the client of the characteristics of some powerful person in the client's early life. It depends, too, on the worker's ability to control his own conscious attitudes toward the client, his liking, his approval or his distaste, his boredom or exasperation or sympathy. Even more, it depends on the worker's ability to pull into consciousness his own subterranean emotions that are a countertransference to the client's transference. The relationship depends on the worker's ability to understand the client's unspoken, perhaps unconscious, emotional needs, and on the worker's willingness to regard the client as an individual with a voice in his own affairs, with an ability to cooperate in planning for his life even if circumstances are forcing him into an unwelcome situation.

So we turn now to the last chapter of this book, a chapter which summarizes the skills, the information, the qualities beyond good intentions which the worker needs.

CHAPTER XIX

More than kind intent

CASEWORK, to be effective, must be practical, understanding, and nonjudgmental—and this involves more in the way of skill and information than might at first appear.

If he is to give practical help the worker must have at his finger tips knowledge about a wide variety of community resources. He may be called on to supply his client with improved housing or necessary medical care, or to help him apply for Social Security or a grant of public assistance, or he may have to arrange special training for a handicapped client, or prenatal care for an unmarried pregnant girl. He may have to advise a client about the legal procedures for securing state hospitalization for a mentally ill relative or a mentally retarded child. He may have to help make out a petition of neglect so that a court will remove a child from an abusive or neglectful home.

But even more than knowledge of resources, a caseworker must have skill to discover the client's actual need. People who ask for help do not always tell the whole truth about their situations, perhaps because they do not have any way of knowing all the facts (about the extent or implications of a mental illness, for instance), perhaps because they do not understand the need for accuracy (in giving residential information to establish eligibility for some types of public assistance, for example). Or it could be that the truth is too painful for the client to face. He may not be able to reveal to a stranger whom he does not yet trust the embarrassing circumstances that have created his need. He may not be able to face facts himself, let alone talk about them. Perhaps he is deluding himself into a belief that things are better than they really are, or he may be trying to persuade himself that his own capacities are greater than the record indicates, or that his own motives and impulses are more admirable than they actually are.

To get at the true facts, a caseworker must have considerable skill in interviewing. He must be able to set his client at ease, make him feel accepted, so that he will be able to relate the more humiliating circumstances of his situation without loss of "face." Although an experienced caseworker will recognize the existence of his client's protective defenses, he will look behind them without demolishing them. A client whose defenses have been torn away abruptly will be far less able to carry on in any practical fashion than he would have been if the worker had permitted him to continue in the shelter of his rationalizations. After all, a worker's purpose is not to prove that he knows everything there is to know about his client, but to make it possible for the client to operate effectively.

Although a caseworker must be practical, he cannot afford to be too literal. If he tries to give help only on the surface level of need which the client is able to express in words, he will sometimes find himself failing dismally. An emotionally starved woman who says, "My child could never bear to leave me" may really mean, "I could never bear to be separated from my child." If the caseworker takes her words literally and proves that the child can very well get along apart from his mother, he will certainly encounter one obstacle after another from this woman. What is needed here is not help to persuade the child to go willingly to hospital or school or camp or wherever he should go, but help to give the mother strength to face the separation. Only if the caseworker understands, will he know which end of the problem to tackle.

In any casework situation the understanding must be a matter of the head as well as of the heart. It cannot be faked, and it is by no means synonymous with sympathy, that amorphous, easy emotion which is frequently more harmful than helpful. Understanding does not come from "putting yourself in the client's place"—you are not the same individual as the client, and you would probably respond quite differently to the same situation. A caseworker's golden rule might be amended to read, "Do unto others as you

would have others do unto you—if you were exactly like that other."
But you are not, of course. Individuality is made up of a combination of the physical, the mental, the emotional. It is the result of the functioning of the glands, and the arteries, and all the physical organs. It is the outcome of all the decisions and beliefs prompted by the inborn mental capacity plus the training and experience the mind has had. It is the response prompted by the emotions, conscious and unconscious, and they in turn are the result of physical and intellectual experiences, plus the habits, the reactions, the conscience, the attitudes toward good and bad, desirable or undesirable, that have developed through the years. In this world of infinite variety no two people are ever exactly alike. So the caseworker cannot be like the client, and the worker would not feel the same as the client feels, nor react in exactly the same way, even if their external circumstances were identical.

It is the client who must be understood. The more a caseworker knows of the forces that shape personality development, the more he is aware of the "common human needs," the more tools he will have at his command to facilitate understanding. The more he is alert to the comforting mechanisms of defense, the less likely he is to be misled by a façade, and the more able to fathom the impulses, the hungers, the urges, that the client must forever try to conceal in order to preserve his own self-respect. Defense mechanisms are necessary. They keep humanity in good working order. No good caseworker will feel that he is obliged to explain a client's defenses to the client, but the worker must be aware that they exist, accept them quietly, look past them to understand the kind of help that is needed.

In addition to understanding the client, any worker must make a thoroughly honest effort to know himself. There are personality traits, perhaps all right in themselves, that are admirable in some situations but disadvantageous in casework. For example, *must* the worker be the one through whom good comes? Anyone finds pleasure in playing Lord or Lady Bountiful, but if it is all-important to a person that *he* be the Giver of All Good, then he may well find it difficult to relinquish a relationship with a client who has been for a time dependent on him. He may even, without realizing it, find subtle ways to sabotage a client's efforts toward independence, persuading himself always, of course, that it is his own fine generosity that makes him prolong the satisfaction of giving.

Anyone finds it more agreeable to be liked than to be disliked, but if it is so terribly important to find approval that one cannot face the unpleasant task of denying something to another, even when that something may in the long run be harmful, then one is not a caseworker. Such a person would yield to the temptation to provide what the client requests, and then contrive some presentable excuse that will persuade the world that he is doing it out of generous concern for the client. Rationalization is easy and it is a universal human defense, but it is not an indulgence appropriate to a giving person in his professional capacity.

This type of unrealistic sympathy, of giving to satisfy the worker's need rather than the client's, is bad. It is always what the client needs, that determines the casework plan—not what the caseworker might find it pleasant to give. And that brings us to another trait that a caseworker should not have. He should never be too impetuously certain just what is best for somebody else. Different people feel differently, and the caseworker must be both willing and able to find out how the client feels.

The understanding, moreover, must be of the individual personality—not of the category only. We have spoken in this book of casework for the child in foster care, for the unmarried mother, for the aged, the handicapped, the mentally retarded. What we learn about one category helps us to work efficiently with another individual in that category, but we must never forget that it *is* another individual. With each aged person we help, we learn something of the physiology and perhaps the psychology of age. With each unmarried mother, we learn more about problems of these girls and about the resources available to help them. But each individual reacts in her own unique fashion to his circumstances, and each must be accepted and understood as an individual.

A worker must be nonjudgmental. Antisocial behavior must be controlled for the safety of society and of the client, but every plan the worker makes must be made in an effort to help the client relate in a better and more productive fashion to his circumstances

—never to punish him for his past undesirable behavior. A child who persistently sets fires must be put where he can set no more fires—not as punishment for being naughty, but to protect society and to keep the child safe while other interests and other habits are instilled into him. If a parent has neglected his children, we may apply to the court for an order that will remove the children from his custody—not to punish the parent but to save the children. If we can work with the parent toward a better relationship with his family without removing the children, we would do so. Punishment of a misbehaving client may relieve the worker's aggravation, but it does not often change the client's behavior over any long period of time.

A caseworker must have self-awareness. Without a knowledge of his own prejudices, his own pet hates, his biases, he may easily distort his picture of the client's personality and betray the reality of the client's situation. Self-awareness is not easy to acquire, and when acquired is often painful. But it is essential that the worker have it.

If a person has not self-awareness, if he has no skill in human relationships, or if he has not the willingness to acquire these qualities, he should never try to be a caseworker. Perhaps he is not suited to social work. Some people are not, and there are other ways in which one can contribute richly to the happiness of mankind. But no one lacking these qualities, or the willingness to acquire them, should embark on any career that involves working with the lives of other individuals.

Helping people wisely is not easy. Understanding is not simple. Self-awareness sometimes hurts. Often complete success is impossible. Nevertheless, the effort to understand and to help is rewarding, both to the one who understands and to the one who is understood even in part. But to provide help which is practical, understanding, and nonjudgmental demands more than kind intent.

Suggested reading

This bibliography can make no pretense of being complete. New and valuable material on mental health, psychology, casework techniques, and related subjects is appearing all the time. The list which follows can do no more than include some of the titles which have come to the author's attention and which would seem to be useful to the person wishing to understand the casework approach.

Group I

The first group consists of books on the general subject of mental and emotional health. They are all written for the interested layman who may have little or no acquaintance with psychiatric terminology. The books in this group can be read with equal value by either the experienced or the novice caseworker.

Baruch, Dorothy W. Personal Problems of Everyday Life. New York, Appleton-Century-Crofts, 1941.
   Presents the practical aspects of mental hygiene as applied to normal and healthy individuals. Interesting and helpful.
Burnham, William. Wholesome Personality. New York, Appleton, 1932.
   Portrays the characteristics of the healthy adult personality. Although it was written more than twenty-five years ago there is much in it of value to the student of psychology today.
Fraiberg, Selma H. The Magic Years. New York, Charles Scribner's Sons, 1959.
   A vivid account of the emotional and intellectual growth of a child from birth through the preschool years. Completely nontechnical. Offers suggestions for the tactful handling of tensions and behavior problems, presenting things with a sensitive understanding of the child's point of view. Gives incidents from the reactions of actual

children observed by the author. Not a complete reference book such as Dr. Spock has provided, but one that is most helpful to a parent, or to anyone who wants to understand what small children need and why they need it.

Guntrip, Harry, J. S. Psychology for Ministers and Social Workers. London, Independent Press, 1951.

Practical and readable presentation of psychology as applied to the art of helping people.

Menninger, Karl. The Human Mind. Garden City, N.Y., Garden City Publishing Co., 1930.

Study of the development of mental reactions and perceptions.

—— Love against Hate. New York, Harcourt Brace & Co., 1942.

Analysis of the causes of human antagonisms, and the ways of creating a social environment less encouraging to hate than to love.

Overstreet, Harry. The Mature Mind. New York, W. W. Norton, 1949.

An analysis of the characteristics of maturity with suggestions for ways to create a national climate conducive to maturity.

Overstreet, Harry, and Bonaro Overstreet. The Mind Alive. New York, W. W. Norton, 1954.

A presentation in clear and simple terms of the meaning of therapy and its benefits to the healthy mind.

Preston, George H. Psychiatry for the Curious. New York, Farrar and Rinehart, 1940.

A simple explanation of the principles of psychiatry.

Group II

The second group of titles is concerned with the problems which may arise in our efforts to help children of various age groups. These books are all written in clear, nontechnical language for the parent, teacher, or group leader, and will be helpful to them whether or not they have special training.

Baruch, Dorothy W. How to Live with Your Teen-Ager. New York, McGraw-Hill Book Co., 1953.

Down-to-earth approach to the emotional problems of adolescence and how a parent can understand and cope with them.

Josselyn, Irene M., M.D. The Happy Child; a Psychoanalytical Guide to Emotional and Social Growth. New York, Random House, 1956.

Written for intelligent parents rather than for teachers or caseworkers.

It presents in simpler terms much the same material as that in the author's *Psychosocial Development of Children.*

—— The Adolescent and His World. New York, Family Service Association of America, 1952.

A discussion of the psychological problems of adolescence. Clear and readable.

Lane, Howard. Human Relations in Teaching. New York, Prentice-Hall, 1955.

Mental hygiene as applied by the teacher in her schoolroom. Offers good suggestions although it is not very detailed in the diagnosis of the problems presented.

Ribble, Margaret A., M.D. Rights of Infants. New York, Columbia University Press, 1943.

A description of the kind of care needed by infants from birth on, emphasizing the importance of handling, cuddling, and rocking, with sound physiological bases supporting each suggestion. It throws a fresh illumination on the frequently repeated statement that each baby needs his own mother-person.

Spock, Benjamin, M.D. Common Sense Book of Baby Care. New York, Duell, Sloan & Pearce, 1945. Also available in paperback edition published by Cardinal Giant, New York.

Gives instructions for parents who want their child to develop normally both physically and emotionally. Takes the child from infancy through the age of seven. Presents material in simple, down-to-earth, sometimes humorous language, but with a solid background knowledge of personality structure. Excellent for any mother, and helpful to a teacher or to anyone working with young children or to those working with the parents of young children.

Wittenberg, Rudolph. So You Want to Help People. New York, Association Press, 1947.

Helpful to anyone interested in group work with children. Gives an interpretation of some types of childhood behavior, with suggestions of how to deal with it in group situations. Also indicates the personality necessary for a successful group leader.

Group III

These books are written for people interested in the development of casework services. A reading from this group would provide some orientation for individuals starting work in either public or private agencies.

Cowgill, Ella Lee. A Guidebook for Beginners in Public Assistance. New York, Family Service Association of America, 1940.

A description of some of the emotional and situational problems met by workers in public assistance programs. Includes some practical suggestions for dealing with the problems. Good reading for anyone interested in public assistance, either as an employee of an agency or as a member of the general public.

Faatz, Anita J. The Nature of Policy and Administration of Public Assistance. Philadelphia, Pennsylvania School of Social Work, 1943.

Describes the aims and the methods applicable to public assistance in the years following the Social Security Act of 1935.

Fink, Arthur. The Field of Social Work. New York, Henry Holt, 1942.

Presents a history of the development of social work practices with an analysis of the contributions of the various agencies in the field up to the date of the writing.

Leyendecker, Hilary. Problems and Policy in Public Assistance. New York, Harper, 1955.

A readable history of the development of social work in this country, and a clear presentation of the current organization dealing with public welfare. Chapters 10, "Social Investigations," and 11, "Human Relations in the Administration of Public Assistance," especially recommended to those interested in casework with the underprivileged.

Rich, Margaret. A Belief in People. New York, Family Service Association of America, 1956.

History of the changing concepts of casework, emphasizing the personalities who have been influential in the thinking and the organizations that have helped formulate present-day methods. More concerned with private than public agencies. Good reading and up to date.

Schneider, David M., and Albert Deutsch. History of Public Assistance in New York. Chicago, University of Chicago Press, 1941.

Detailed and accurate history of welfare in New York State up to 1940.

Group IV

These books and pamphlets are somewhat more technical than any of those in the preceding groups. The writers assume an interest in the psychiatric approach to an understanding of human behavior. The terminology, however, can be understood by the beginner in casework.

Bowlby, John. Child Care and the Growth of Love. Baltimore, Penguin Books, 1957.

A summary of a report prepared under the auspices of the World Health Organization in 1951 on the importance of mother love in the development of a child's character. Emphasizes the theory that lack of continuous care by a mother-person during the first year results in a personality that is unable to give or accept affection.

Community Service Society. Social Work as Human Relations. New York, Columbia University Press, 1949.

A collection of articles by different authors. The articles are grouped under headings: "Theory and Techniques," "Professional Training," "Vistas in Human Relations."

English, O. Spurgeon, M.D., and Stuart Finch, M.D. Introduction to Psychiatry. New York, W. W. Norton & Co., 1954.

Can be read without previous acquaintance with psychiatry. Describes behavior patterns in a way helpful to anyone interested in understanding human behavior.

English, O. Spurgeon, M.D., and Gerald Pearson, M.D. Emotional Problems of Living. New York, W. W. Norton & Co., 1955; rev. ed.

Well written, combining technical accuracy with smooth presentation so that the book is easy to read; helpful to the beginning as well as to the advanced student. This revision incorporates many useful suggestions made by practicing social workers, teachers, psychologists. It is a balanced study of the emotional problems encountered from infancy to old age.

—— Common Neuroses of Children and Adults. New York, W. W. Norton & Co., 1937.

A most complete presentation of the psychiatric approach to human behavior, geared to the understanding of any intelligent reader. Previous acquaintance with psychiatry is not necessary to benefit by this book.

French, Thomas M., M.D. Psychoanalytic Orientation in Casework. New York, Family Service Association of America, 1944.

This pamphlet contains two articles. Dr. French presents reasons why any caseworker should have some knowledge of the psychiatric interpretation of personality problems, and Ralph Ormsby describes a case history which was successful because of the worker's awareness of psychiatric interpretations.

Hall, Calvin. A Primer of Freudian Psychology. Cleveland, World Publishing Company, 1954.

A fairly simple presentation of the Freudian theories of personality structure. Reprinted in paperback edition by Mentor Books in the New American Library of World Literature, New York.

Hamilton, Gordon. Psychotherapy in Child Guidance. New York, Columbia University Press, 1947.
Clear and workmanlike. Does not suffer appreciably from the passage of time since the date of publication.
—— Theory and Practice of Social Case Work. New York, Columbia University Press, 1940; 2d ed., 1951.
The new edition brings theories and practices up to date. A thorough and valuable contribution to the philosophy of casework.
Horney, Karen. Our Inner Conflicts. New York, W. W. Norton & Co., 1954.
Analysis of the various types of conflicts and fears to which humans are subject. Organization of material is somewhat different from that used in the Freudian system of personality development since Miss Horney is of the Rankian school.
Josselyn, Irene M., M.D. Psychosocial Development of Children. New York, Family Service Association of America, 1948.
A clear and readable presentation of the Freudian theory of personality structure, with an analysis of the motivations prompting childhood behavior. It is geared to the reader of professional caliber who has no profound preknowledge of psychiatry. A very valuable book for any caseworker who needs to understand children.
Noyes, Arthur, P., M.D. Modern Clinical Psychiatry. Philadelphia, W. B. Saunders Co., 1948.
An excellent text in the diagnosis of psychoses. Written with clinical detail. Can be understood without previous knowledge of psychiatry but is not light reading.
Redl, Fritz. Mental Hygiene in Teaching. New York, Harcourt Brace & Co., 1951; 2d ed., 1959.
Describes behavior mechanisms, some personality distortions, and offers warnings to teachers working with upset children.
Rogers, Carl. Counseling and Psychotherapy. Boston and New York, Houghton Mifflin, 1942.
A readable and detailed book dealing with the causation of human behavior and methods of influencing the behavior. Includes considerable case material and sample interviews.
Saul, Leon. Emotional Maturity; the Development and Dynamics of Personality. Philadelphia and New York, 1947.
Analysis of personality characteristics that denote maturity. Good reading, provocative of thought.
Snyder, William. Casebook of Non-directive Counseling. Boston and New York, Houghton Mifflin, 1947.

Verbatim records of interviews, with running comments and criticisms of the interviewing techniques. Excellent as a study of counseling and of types of direct interviews.

Towle, Charlotte. Common Human Needs. New York, National Association of Social Workers, 1945; rev., 1952 and 1957.

Written as a guide to beginning public assistance workers, but valuable to anyone planning to work with people in need. Outlines the significance of public assistance for the individual and for society. Lists and discusses the common human needs at each stage of development, from infancy through childhood, adulthood, and old age. Also discusses the needs of the handicapped and the needs of a family group.

Young, Leontine. Out of Wedlock. New York, McGraw-Hill Book Co., 1954.

A study of the psychological motivations for out-of-wedlock pregnancies, and some suggestions for working with unmarried mothers. Important for anyone who may be in a position to guide and help such girls.

Zachry, Caroline. Personality Adjustment of School Children. New York, Charles Scribners, 1929.

Series of case histories of difficult children. Especially good for the studies of family history and background. Rather superficial in discussion of treatment of the problems and shows no knowledge of Freudian theories, but excellent for its suggestions for methods of gathering case material.

Group V

The following books and pamphlets show the caseworker at work. Resources and techniques are discussed in relation to specific situations.

Baruch, Dorothy W. One Little Boy. New York, Julian Press, 1952.
Detailed case history of work with a disturbed boy in play therapy. Excellent for showing the conflicts in this child and the way he was helped. Also gives a vivid picture of the way in which play therapy operates.

Bettelheim, Bruno. Love Is Not Enough. Glencoe, Ill., Free Press, 1950.
An interesting account of the day-by-day work done with disturbed children in the Orthogenic School in Chicago. Helpful in understanding normal children as well as those sufficiently upset to need specialized care.

Bettelheim, Bruno. Truants from Life. Glencoe, Ill., Free Press, 1955.
Detailed studies of work with four children in the Orthogenic School
in Chicago. A model of clinical reporting which still manages to carry
strong human interest throughout.

Bowers, Swithun, O.M.I. Nature and definition of Social Casework.
Family Service Association of America, 1949.
A most valuable article, which presents a number of definitions of
casework, arranged chronologically to show changing concepts of
casework. The second part of the article is a thought-provoking discussion of the possibilities open to casework today.

Charnley, Jean. The Art of Child Placement. Minneapolis, University of
Minnesota Press, 1955.
A sympathetic and practical approach to the emotional problems of
children removed from their own homes to be placed in foster homes,
or institutions, valuable for anyone working with children who are
living apart from their own families. Should be helpful to teachers,
group leaders, or others who come in contact with children in other
than normal family conditions.

Fraiberg, Selma H. Psychoanalytical Principles in Casework with Children. New York, Family Service Association of America, 1955.
This pamphlet contains four articles, all readable and interesting and
each illustrating the light which a knowledge of psychiatric principles
throws on the problems of childhood behavior.

Garrett, Annette. Interviewing: Its Principles and Methods. New York,
Family Service Association of America, 1942.
A good presentation of the technique of interviewing. Includes a
number of illustrative interviews with analyses of the methods used
in each.

Gerard, Margaret, M.D. The Emotionally Disturbed Child. New York,
Child Welfare League of America, 1956.
The book consists of ten parts originally published in a variety of
places over the last ten years. They all emphasize the psychobiological
aspects of behavior and discuss the problems related to work with
disturbed children. Accurate, professional, and readable.

Glickman, Esther. Child Placement through Clinically Oriented Casework. New York, Columbia University Press, 1957.
The author studies the types of foster homes, institutions, and residential treatment centers available for children who must be separated from their own families. She discusses the need for an under-

standing in each situation of personality structure, past and present deprivations, defenses, ego strength and weaknesses, current social reality, before a wise choice of placement can possibly be made for any child.

Gordon, Henrietta L. Casework Services for Children. Boston, Houghton Mifflin, 1956.

Systematic presentation of the casework services for children, including boarding home care, institutional care, adoption, day care, supervision in the child's own home, supervised homemaking services.

Hamilton, Gordon. Psychotherapy in Child Guidance. New York, Columbia University Press, 1947.

In this book Miss Hamilton shows in what ways psychotherapy is related to social work. Child guidance is here assumed to call for the integration of educational, social, and therapeutic principles.

Hamilton, Gordon, and Hyman Grossbard. Developing Self-Awareness. New York, Family Association of America, 1954.

This pamphlet presents two articles reprinted from *Social Casework*, November, 1954. Both discuss the caseworker's need for self-awareness and the methods by which such awareness can be developed on the job.

Hartley, Ruth E., *et al.* Understanding Children's Play. New York, Columbia University Press, 1952.

Discusses the recorded observations of psychologists involved in a project to explore the potentialities of play materials for understanding children in nursery and kindergarten groups.

Hutchinson, Dorothy. In Quest of Foster Parents. New York, Columbia University Press, 1943.

Describes the needs of foster children and the services that foster parents can give to children. Indicates the qualities required for successful work with foster children.

Kasius, Cora, ed. New Directions in Social Work. New York, Harper, 1954.

Fifteen leading authorities on social work examine such recent developments as the expansion of government activity in the area of welfare, the increasingly international scope of social work, new concepts in professional education, new problems and policies in the organization and finance of volunteer agencies and the role of social work in social reform.

—— Principles and Techniques in Social Casework. New York, Family Service Association of America, 1950.

A series of articles on subjects related to work in welfare agencies. The articles are grouped under headings: "Philosophy," "Teaching and Supervision," "Practice." A valuable book for anyone interested in professional casework.

Kempshall, Anna, ed. Child Therapy: a Casework Symposium. New York, Family Service Association of America, 1948.

A series of practical and valuable articles by teachers and practicing caseworkers on the subject of work with disturbed children.

Lowrey, Lawson G., ed. Psychiatry for Social Workers. New York, Columbia University Press, 1950; 2d ed.

Outlines the type of information about the client required for any useful study of a disturbed person. Lists the economic, social, etiological data to be considered. Factual and clear.

Lowry, Fern, ed. Readings in Social Case Work, 1920–1938. New York, Columbia University Press, 1939.

Selected reprints of articles appearing between 1920 and 1938. Most of these are still valuable.

Meier, Elizabeth G. The Foster Care of Children with Psychotic Mothers. New York, Child Welfare League of America, 1955.

Discusses the early damage done to children by psychotic mothers, and the difficulties experienced by caseworkers attempting to help such mothers after the child is placed away from his home. Offers suggestions for rehabilitation.

National Conference on Social Welfare. Social Welfare Forum. New York, Columbia University Press, 1957.

Reprints of more than twenty papers originally presented at the 1957 Annual Forum of the National Conference on Social Welfare where the theme was "Expanding Frontiers in Social Welfare." All the articles are stimulating and thought-provoking. This conference has been meeting annually since 1874, and each year their publications offer much of value.

O'Connell, Marie H. Foster Home Services for Children. New York, Child Welfare League of America, 1955.

Suggests ways in which a child can be helped to accept and use foster home care.

Page, Norma Knoll. Protective Services: a Case Illustrating Casework with Parents. New York, Child Welfare League of America, 1955.

A detailed discussion of a family situation handled by an authoritative agency which had been asked by the court to supervise a home because the parents were neglectful. Shows the possibilities for rehabilitation in a situation which at first seemed hopeless and in which the parents were initially most resistive.

Parad, Howard J., ed. Ego Psychology and Dynamic Casework. New York, Family Service Association of America, 1958.

These papers were written with the aim of examining the impact of ego psychology on casework practice and of relating casework theory to new developments in the social sciences. Variations in points of view are forthrightly expressed.

Peck, Harris B., M.D. Treatment of the Delinquent Adolescent. Family Service Association of America, 1954.

A realistic picture of the difficulties and successes in the use of psychotherapeutic techniques with delinquent adolescents.

Perlman, Helen Harris. Social Casework: a Problem-solving Process. Chicago, University of Chicago Press, 1957.

An excellent analysis of the casework approach to helping people cope with their problems. Geared for people associated with a social work agency, or at least acquainted with the functioning of such agencies. Readable and valuable for anyone who wants to help people.

Raymond, Louise. Adoption and After. New York, Harper, 1955.

Outlines the services which adoption agencies can offer to adoptive parents and to children eligible for adoptive placement. Several excellent chapters on what to expect of children who have been uprooted by separation from natural parents, on how to tell a child he is adopted, and how to answer questions about the birth process.

Richmond, Mary. Social Diagnosis. New York, Russell Sage Foundation, 1917.

An important landmark in the progress of social thinking. Contains material still pertinent although the book was written more than forty years ago.

Robinson, Virginia. Changing Psychology in Social Work. Boston and New York, Houghton Mifflin Co., 1939.

One of the best presentations of the techniques of therapy, with some good suggestions for effective interviewing.

Rall, Mary E., and Esther Glickman. Working with the Child and His Parents. New York, Child Welfare League of America, 1954.

Two articles, one concerning casework in a child's own home, one concerning treatment after placement in foster care.

Ross, Helen, and Adelaide H. Johnson, M.D. Psychiatric Interpretation of the Growth Process. New York, Family Service Association of America, 1949.

Two articles outlining briefly and clearly the Freudian concept of personality structure and the influences that affect personality development.

Simcox, Beatrice R., and Irving Kaufman, M.D. *Character Disorders in Parents of Delinquents.* New York, Family Service Association of America, 1959. An analysis of the character disorders found in parents of delinquents, with suggestions of how to work with these people.

Group VI

These titles present theory for the more advanced reader.

Apteker, Herbert H. Dynamics of Casework Counseling. Boston and New York, Houghton Mifflin, 1955.
Leads the reader persuasively from a brief historical résumé of the origin and evolution of casework as a method of providing social services to a discussion of the two philosophies current today (Freudian and Rankian). Discusses the differences between casework counseling, counseling, and psychotherapy.

Bender, Lauretta, M.D. Aggressions, Hostility, and Anxiety in Children. Springfield, Ill., Charles C. Thomas, 1953.
Case studies of children under observation in the Children's Service of the Psychiatric Division of Bellevue Hospital through 1934–35. Valuable in helping toward a better understanding of disturbed children and the symptoms which indicate deep-seated disturbances. Somewhat specialized in that it discusses such extreme symptoms as concern with death, suicidal tendencies, homicidal aggression, fire-setting.

Bradley, Charles. Schizophrenia in Childhood. New York, Macmillan, 1941.
Historical survey of the literature of schizophrenia and quotations of the varying opinions concerning incidence and symptomatology of the disease.

Cronbach, Lee J. Essentials of Psychological Testing. New York, Harper, 1949.
Detailed descriptions of the several types of testing both for mental diagnosis and for personality.

Eissler, Ruth, *et al.*, eds. The Psychoanalytic Study of the Child. New York, International Universities Press, 1945.
A volume of this title has appeared annually from 1945 up to and including 1959. The publication is expected to continue as an annual. Each volume is a very important collection of the clinical and theo-

retical papers which have appeared in professional journals. Together the books provide an invaluable picture of the developing psychoanalytical knowledge of child development. Some of the papers are reports of technical research of interest chiefly to trained analysts, but most of them can be read with understanding and benefit by any interested person who has some background knowledge of personality structure.

Fenichel, Otto. Psychoanalytical Theory of the Neuroses. New York, W. W. Norton, 1945.

Accurate and professional, geared to a reader with some knowledge of psychiatry.

Freud, Anna. The Ego and the Mechanisms of Defense. New York, International Universities Press, 1946.

Rather technical, but very much worth reading for one with some previous acquaintance with Freudian theories.

Hyman, Herbert H., *et al.* Interviewing in Social Research. Chicago, University of Chicago Press, 1955.

A reexamination of the interviewing techniques in an effort to determine the relationship between the interviewer and the person interviewed. Reports are included on new experimental and field studies.

Kasius, Cora, ed. A Comparison of Diagnostic and Functional Casework Concepts. New York, Family Service Association of America, 1950.

Includes case studies handled in accord with each of the current schools, Freudian and Rankian.

Lewis, Nolan, and Bernard Pacella, eds. Modern Trends in Child Psychology. New York, International Universities Press, 1945.

Collection of professional articles written by and for psychologists.

Rambert, Madeleine. Children in Conflict; Twelve Years of Psychoanalytic Practice. New York, International Universities Press, 1949.

Describes types of resistance seen in disturbed children and outlines the sort of background material necessary before a diagnosis can be determined. Also gives a good description of play therapy.

Redl, Fritz, and David Wineman. Children Who Hate. Glencoe, Ill., Free Press, 1951.

—— Controls from Within. Glencoe, Ill., Free Press, 1952.

Both these titles describe work with disturbed children, giving suggestions for diagnosis and treatment.

Slavson, S. R. Child Psychotherapy. New York, Columbia University Press, 1952.

Clinical studies with special emphasis on treatment of emotionally disturbed children under twelve. Follows the Freudian theory of personality development. Explicit and quite technical.

Small, S. Mouchly, M.D. Symptoms of Personality Disorder. New York, Family Welfare Association of America, 1945.

Description of behavior patterns which might alert one to the possibility of a psychosis developing. Shows the difference between psychotic and psychopathic personalities.

Sterba, Richard, *et al.* Transference in Casework. New York, Family Service Association of America, 1949.

Three authors, Richard Sterba, M.D., Benjamin H. Lyndon, and Anna Katz, discuss the dangers inherent in the transference situation and offer suggestions of the ways in which this emotional reaction can be used in the most beneficial way.

Group VII

Books in this last group include biography, autobiography, and fiction. The biographies and autobiographies concern themselves with the experiences and reactions of individuals who have had intimate and personal contact with mental illness. Some of the fiction provide sensitive interpretation of human problems; other titles listed are in a lighter vein of entertainment. Fiction written with a sound basis of knowledge may give considerable insight into human troubles and the means by which they may be aggravated or solved. Even the lighter stories often provide a fleeting glimpse that suggests a fresh point of view, and it is on such a basis that the titles were selected. Again it must be emphasized that neither this list nor the professional titles of the preceding lists can make any pretense of being complete. A number of other titles will no doubt suggest themselves to the reader. But if this bibliography starts the novice caseworker reading for a surer grasp of human motivations and a wider knowledge of how to help, it will have served its purpose.

Aldington, Richard. Death of a Hero. Chicago, Covici-Friede, 1929.

George begins early to feel worthless and incapable of achievement. All through his life the feeling pursues him. What he does because of the frustrations created by his early environment makes a classical tale.

Armstrong, Charlotte. Dram of Poison. New York, Howard McCann, 1956.

A suspense story, written probably as pure entertainment, but in addition to telling an exciting story, the book gives a vivid picture of the near-tragic damage which may follow the attempts of an obtuse person to apply superficial and inadequate knowledge of psychiatry to the lives of others.

Aswell, Mary Louise, ed. The World Within. New York, McGraw-Hill Book Co., 1947.
A collection of short stories illuminating the neuroses of our time. The authors from whose works selections are made date from Hoffman, who died in 1822, to Faulkner. All of the tales are concerned with abnormal personalities.

Bassing, Eileen. Home before Dark. New York, Random House, 1957.
The deeply understanding story of the efforts made by a woman recently a patient in a hospital for the mentally ill to adjust in the community.

Beers, Clifford W. A Mind That Found Itself. New York, Doubleday, Doran & Co., 1935.
An autobiographical account of the experiences of a man hospitalized as a manic-depressive. Important for the picture it gives of institutions of that time, and for the great influence it had in correcting abuse and carelessness in the treatment of the mentally ill.

Bottome, Phyllis. Jane. New York, Vanguard Press, 1957.
The story of a delinquent. Gives a sensitive picture of the influences in Jane's life which resulted in her behavior, and a vivid picture of the attitudes she faced from the various social agencies with which she came in contact.

—— Private Worlds. Boston and New York, Houghton Mifflin, 1934.
Story shows how tenuous and slim are the barriers between behavior indicative of sanity and insanity.

Brand, Millen. The Outward Room. New York, Simon and Schuster, 1937.
Fiction, possibly tinged with biography. The story of a girl who escapes from a mental hospital and then with the help of another person's tenderness, gains insight into her own needs, becoming eventually a more complete and a healthier individual.

Brown, Carlton. Brainstorm. New York, Farrar and Rinehart, 1944.
Autobiography. Pictures a man's symptoms and attitudes at the time of the onset and throughout the duration of a mental illness. Lacks objectivity, as might be expected. Must be read as a study of the symptoms as though one were, in fact, observing the behavior of a mentally ill patient.

Hillyer, Jane. Reluctantly Told. New York, Macmillan, 1927.
Autobiography. A girl, hospitalized as manic-depressive, depressed

phase, gives a vivid and poignant account of her period of despair and of how she finds herself and her sanity.

Kuttner, Henry. The Murder of Ann Avery. New York, Permabook, 1956.
—— The Murder of Eleanor Pope. New York, Permabook, 1956.
Both these stories are, as the titles indicate, murder tales of the "who-dunit" type. Their value to the reader interested in psychiatry rests in the fact that the protagonist is a psychoanalyst and that the descriptions of his interviews with the suspected murderer present an authentic picture of an analyst's approach.

Leader, Pauline. And No Birds Sing. New York, Vanguard Press, 1931.
Story of a sensitive girl whose parents punish her severely. She grows deaf, and one senses this to be not only the result of illness but also of her desire to escape from constant threats and condemnation.

Lincoln, Victoria. February Hill. New York, Farrar and Rinehart, 1934.
The story of a family from the wrong side of the tracks. Gives a realistic portrayal of the attitudes and loyalties of people whose behavior might well be criticized as antisocial but whose standards are as firm and in many ways as admirable as those of persons whose actions are more conventional.

Lindner, Robert. Fifty Minute Hour. New York, Rinehart, 1955.
Five stories told by a professional psychoanalyst based on material learned from his analysands during analysis.

Maule, Hamilton. Jeremy Todd. New York, Random House, 1959.
Sensitively told story of a boy's emotional reaction to the death of a beloved grandfather who had stood in a father's place in this boy's life. Provides considerable insight into a child's near-delinquent behavior as he attempts to work through the loss of the most meaningful person in his life.

Moore, William L. The Mind in Chains. New York, Exposition Press, 1955.
Autobiography. Written while the author was a patient in a mental hospital from 1953 to August, 1954, diagnosed as a schizophrenic, paranoid type. Presents a picture of his life prior to hospitalization as he becomes increasingly separated from reality. Describes in considerable detail his reactions to the electric shock, metrazol, and insulin treatments. Excellent as a clinical study.

Robinson, Alice Merritt. The Unbelonging. New York, Macmillan, 1958.
Provides understanding of the emotions of an individual struggling to establish contact and relationship with other people.

Ward, Mary Jane. The Snake Pit. New York, Random House, 1946.
Story of a young woman's experiences in a hospital for the mentally

ill. Suggests by implication rather than by any direct criticism some of the mistakes made in the handling and treatment of the patients.

Wexler, Susan Stanhope. The Story of Sandy. New York, Bobbs-Merrill, 1955.

A touching and realistic story of a child deprived of all confidence in his mother's love. Because of this early insecurity the child withdraws into himself, becoming autistic to such a degree that he is believed hopelessly retarded. However, slow, patient, loving care on the part of his foster parents effect considerable improvement. The story is said to be true, and it sounds authentic.

Wilson, Donald Powell. My Six Convicts. New York, Rinehart, 1951.

A report given with sympathy, understanding, and some touches of humor, of the experiences of a psychologist working with six criminals in a prison setting.

Index

Garrett, Annette, cited, 23n, 39; quoted, 146

Geriatric caseworker, 141; *see also* Aged, the

Group work: with adolescents, 97, 99; suggested readings on, 160-61

Guidance counselors: adolescents and, 99; need of casework techniques, 2-3, 9

Handicapped, the, 3, 67; husband-wife relationship in handicapped cases, 112; need for understanding of, as individuals, 156; relationship of caseworker with, 111, 115, 116, with parents of, 113-14; suggested readings on, 165; training for, 153; types of services available for, 70-71; *see* Mentally retarded; Physically handicapped

Health problems, types of services available, 70

Heterosexuality, 95, 97-98, 126

Hollis, Florence, quoted, 43

Home environment: influence of, 16, 44-45, 85-91 *passim;* neglectful, 153; of retarded children, 104; of unmarried mothers-to-be, 123-24; *see also* Parents

Home relief, 84

Hospital insurance, 140

Hospitalization, 7

Howard, Donald, quoted, 40

Human needs: four basic, 59-65; suggested readings on, 165

Husband-wife relationship, 16, 112

Immaturity in adults, 53-58

Institutionalization: of the aged, 142-43; of delinquent children, 151; of handicapped children, 114-15, 117-18; of illegitimate babies, 124; of mentally retarded children, 106, 108-10, 124, 153; suggested readings on, 166

"Intake process," 66-77, 145

Intellectualization, 9

Interpretation technique, 3, 8-10, 39

Interviewee, *see* Client

Interviewing: skill in, 154; suggested readings on, 166, 171; techniques of, 19-27

Interviews: collateral, 28-32; diagnostic, 33-42; first, 12-18; intake, 66-77; two types of, 28

Judgmental attitudes, *see* Nonjudgmental attitude

Law enforcement agencies, types of services available, 71

Leyendecker, Hilary, quoted, ix, x-xi, 79

Marital relationship, vii, xii, 60, 95

Marriage counseling service, 65

Maturity: characteristics of, 54; in adults, 53-58; reasons for lack of, 55; road to, 95; suggested readings on, 160

Medical care, 65, 69, 139-40; *see also* Doctor

Medical examination, need for, 49

Medical reports, 11

Medical social worker, physically handicapped and, 111

Mental development, 53

Mental health: suggested readings in, 159-75 *passim;* types of services available, 72

Mental hygiene, suggested readings in, 159, 161

Mental illness, 52, 55-58; state hospitalization for, 153; suggested readings on, 172-75; *see also specific forms of,* e.g., Psychosis

Mentally retarded, 104-10; institutionalization of, 106, 108-10, 124, 153; need for understanding of, as individuals, 156; possibility of retardation in child privately adopted, 134; relationship of caseworker with, 108-9, with parents of, 113-14

Ministers, need of casework technique, vii, xii, 2, 3

Mothers, 2, 69, 154, 163; relationship with daughter, 97-98, 124-30; relationship with son, 124-27; *see also* Parents; Unmarried mothers

"Negative transference," 92-93

Neighborhood, standards in, 16, 17

Neuroses, 4, 55-56; in parents of retarded children, 107-8; in pregnant unwed girl, 121-22; psychoanalytical theory of, 171